MVRDV

To Nina and Matteo

Michele Costanzo

MVRDV
Works and Projects 1991–2006

Cover
Mirador, Sanchinarro, 2001–04.
View of the terrace

Flap
Silodam, Amsterdam, 1995–2002.
Detail of the west façade

Back flap
Mirador, Sanchinarro, 2001–04

Editor
Luca Molinari

Design
Marcello Francone

Editing
Laura Guidetti

Layout
Paola Ranzini

Translations
Marco Migotto and Robert Burns, Language
Consulting Congressi S.r.l., Milan
(from Italian into English)

First published in Italy in 2006 by
Skira Editore S.p.A.
Palazzo Casati Stampa
via Torino 61
20123 Milano
Italy
www.skira.net

Printed and bound in Italy. First edition

ISBN-13: 978-88-7624-649-4
ISBN-10: 88-7624-649-5

Distributed in North America by Rizzoli
International Publications, Inc., 300 Park
Avenue South, New York, NY 10010.
Distributed elsewhere in the world by
Thames and Hudson Ltd., 181a High
Holborn, London WC1V 7QX, United
Kingdom.

The author wishes to thank the
MVRDV studio – in particular Winy
Maas and Paula van Baak – for images
and kind assistance during
the creation of this book.

Contents

Introduction

MVRDV's work may be taken as an emblem of the important turning point in Dutch architecture that came about in the 1990s, initiating a radical transformation of the country in the physical and spatial sense. This grew out of a far-reaching economic, political, social, and ideological (with a new form of democracy based on experimental systems and expanded citizen involvement) reorientation and the profound influence of new and sophisticated communications networks. In sum, it was the affirmation of a new way of relating to the built environment, whose most immediate outcome was the initiation of a significant growth process (especially in housing) that modified, as it were, the country's skyline.

As pointed out by sociologist Ulrick Beck[1], Holland passed from a condition of 'initial modernity' based on the idea of the nation-state, of a society where interpersonal relationships, information networks, and the community are essentially encompassed within territorial limits, and also based on models of collective living, progress, controllability, full employment, and exploitation of nature, to a 'second modernity' which undermined the reassuring but limiting support system in favour of a widely felt need to conquer 'more distant spaces' and which would lead to the reformulation, as extreme consequence, of the very concepts of architecture, urban planning, and landscape. While this new vision theoretically brought with it the need to redefine such notions as *space*, *distance*, *place*, and *habitable environment*, in concrete terms it caused noticeable changes in the city and in the image of the urban landscape.

This transformation in conceptual design criteria and the mechanisms for bringing it into concrete reality expanded to embrace the architectural 'figure' and its capacity to absorb and encompass its constituent elements. One of the outcomes of this process was the configuration of a new formal universe that would illuminate a new grammatical and syntactical freedom.

This innovative thrust would soon transform the Dutch territory into a research laboratory of advanced experimentation on the contemporary city. The country's newest architectural works would become part of its 'second modernity,' which would take form through a profuse series of intriguing and strongly 'anti-dogmatic' works by a large number of young architects. In addition to MVRDV these included Wiel Arets, Ben van Berkel (Un Studio), Erick van Egeraat, Mecanoo, Willem Jan Neutelings, Nox, Kas Oosterhuis, Claus en Kaan, Koen van Velsen, and Adriaan Geuze (West 8). Their creations aroused great interest and favourable reviews in major architectural journals, with no small thanks to the active involvement and influence of Rem Koolhaas, who would call attention—not only on the part of international critics, but also that of the users (usually passive, if not distracted, regarding such topics)—to the aesthetic suggestions of the innovative architectural works. Needless to say, this positive reception would bring significant economic returns.

The process of innovation of the architectonic language would begin in the early 1990s via two important events: the symposium 'Hoe modern is de Nederlandse architectuur?' organised by Koolhaas at the Delft University of Technology in 1990; and the Dutch presence at the Venice Biennial of 1991. The symposium would help a new wave of designers gain awareness of the profound reasons for the crisis of values of their times, develop some perspective on their difficult liaison with the tradition of the modern, and reflect on possible alternative paths. The occasion was marked by a riveting speech by Koolhaas and an equally incisive one by Hans van Dijk, who would coin the expression 'schoolmarm modernism' (which would later become a slogan) to characterise the effete application of the traditionalist cliché of the then recent Dutch architectural production, excluding the vigilant exercise of the individual critical spirit.

The 1991 Venice Biennial[2] would make a significant contribution to clarifying the cultural imprint exemplified by the most recent works, as evinced by the title of the exhibition, 'Modernism without Dogma.' Promoting a new 'non-dogmatic' version of Dutch modernism, the event would seem to provide an indirect response to Van Dijk. As Hans Ibelings pointed out in the exhibition brochure, the last fifty years had seen modern Dutch architecture transformed into a vibrant tradition. Modernism's distinct image between the two world wars along with the range of ideas expressed by the architects of past years had ended up being absorbed by the then current practice of architectural design. The characteristic trait of the newest generation of Dutch architects was their free interpretation of this recent past. For these young creative minds, Modernism, which for them stretched from Duiker to Siza, was an inexhaustible source of free inspiration. The result of this uninhibited behaviour was a modernism without dogma, an inventive modernism imbued with extraordinary formal richness.[3]

[1] Ulrich Beck, 'Reflexive Modernisierung,' in *ARCH+*, no. 143, October 1998.

[2] Ten architecture studios were invited to the event: Wiel Arets/Wim van den Bergh, Jan Benthem/Mels Crouwel; Ben van Berkel; Bert Dirrix/Rein van Wylick; Paul Dobbelaar/Herman de Kovel/Paul de Vroom; Frits van Dongen; Mecanoo; Willem Jan Neutelings/Frank Roodbeen; Jan Pesman; Koen van Velsen.

[3] Hans Ibelings, *Modernism without dogma. A generation of younger architects in the Netherlands*, exhibition brochure, The Hague 1991.

Donau City, Kissing Towers,
Vienna A 2002.
View of the towers

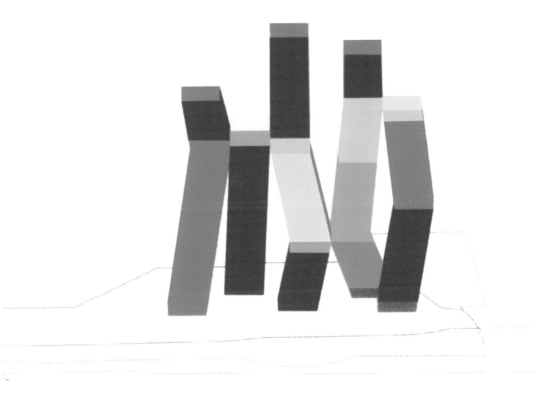

The Developmental Years

Winy Maas, Jacob van Rijs, and Natalie de Vries, after graduating from the Delft University of Technology in 1990 and working with a number of important European architecture studios, participated together in the Europan 2 design contest in 1991, winning first prize for their plan to redevelop a 19th-century Berlin neighbourhood. This immediate success would give them the boost they needed to continue working together under the acronym MVRDV, a name which would soon be known around the world.

A few years later, after much recognition and acclaim, they were asked to give a résumé of their initial experiences at the studios of Martinez Lapeña & Torres in Barcelona, Mecanoo in Delft, and, above all, OMA in Rotterdam. They felt that the most appropriate word to connect their experience with OMA to what they were doing now was 'communication' in a very broad sense. This included a literary culture and broad library resources, involvement with a variety of different people and consultants, and the vast possibilities opened up by the different types of communication medium. This 'communication' gives speed to thought, and given the time it takes to erect buildings and resolve intellectual debates, this speed is fundamental in allowing the architectural profession to move as fast as it does. They also commented on the value of travelling and working in different places both during and after the period of formal studies in terms of enriching perspectives. These work experiences may be considered part of one's education, but when one keeps moving from place to place they simply become part of one's history.[1]

In order to get a fuller picture of the group's formative period it is important to consider the influence of Koolhaas's thought and his role in orienting their choice of goals. In particular, his writings on the contemporary metropolis represent a fundamental theoretical as well as analytical contribution to their development. According to Koolhaas, the metropolis appears to be a disorganised set of contrasting forces devoid of any idea of harmony or composition, where everything exists only to the extent that it differs from the other parts.[2] The only possible design response lies in the ceaseless attempt to overcome all elements of discord through the creation of a new system of logical connections that can unite architectural specificity with programmatic instability. The only option is thus to adhere as closely as possible to reality, purifying oneself of moralisms and preconceptions, exploring and illuminating its inner dynamics and antinomies (recovering even its banal or irrational aspects). An intense interchange with one's context is fundamentally important for grasping the elements that will help one understand it, improve it, and modify it via the project.

Berlin Voids, Berlin 1991.
View of model

13

Koolhaas thus introduces a singular and new proactive approach focused on two rhetorical figures: *exaggeration*, which stimulates the 'reawakening of reality,' bringing what is latent into the light; and *paradox*, which highlights apparent contradictions while containing within itself the hope for a final reconciliation. His conceptual and operative path does not have a formal framework that is clearly defined by a specific aesthetic vision or by functional demands, but rather it tends towards the logic established by the program. This gives rise to an analytical and planning method that derives from the 'casual' objectivity of events that may crop up during one's professional career. According to his markedly 'inclusivist' thought he gives freedom of expression also to the possible contradictions found in client requests or design competitions.

The new Dutch generation (and in particular MVRDV) strongly felt the influence of Koolhaas's ideology and stance on design, and its members did not fail to extend and explore the intrinsic potentials of his approach, feeling out new hypotheses in order to advance along new conceptual and cognitive pathways. In this sense, MVRDV's method, hinging on the application of the *datascape* 'technique'—which may be defined as a manifestation of 'sublimated pragmatism'[3]—once again finds OMA as its point of reference.

Jos Bosman observed that when Winy Maas was working in the Koolhaas studio, one of his special abilities was to develop complex diagrams, sketches, drawings, and other investigations into the reality behind the planning and design strategies. While some sceptically explained Koolhaas's associations as a form of ironic imagination, Maas was actively intent on transforming them—magically, one might say—into a design method.[4]

Their method is based on such a generalised use of data that the very essence of artistic intuition is 'suspended' (in spite of the fact that there is a good degree of decisional freedom as to how to manipulate the acquired elements of knowledge and subsequently translate them into images). They carry out extensive research aimed at assembling an enormous amount of information prior to moving on to the design phase, where the data are selected and interpreted. In this latter phase, the architects make some use of conventional tools of representation (sketches, drawings, models, computer imaging, etc.), which are complemented with statistically composed abstract diagrams, informative graphs, and three-dimensional representations as the final step in the investigation and selection process. In this manner, creativity is not expressed as the invention of new forms, but rather as the exploration and analysis of existing constraints. As notes Stan Allen, an unexpected solution is found by describing the problem in a different way. Form assumes meaning in relation to the information it encodes. Architecture, seen as a series of commutations, circuits, or relays, activates assemblages of data and information; everything is explained, nothing is invented, nothing is arbitrary.[5]

What is particularly attractive about their work is the apparent clarity of the design process, accentuated by the series of diagrammatic drawings that seek to explain the logic of their conceptual pathway. These drawings do not, however, reveal the secrets hidden within the projects, thus leaving room for a host of surprises and sparking the emotional involvement of the beholder or user.

As states Bart Lootsma, the datascape can be thought of as a tool that seeks to identify 'gravitational fields' in the apparent chaos of territorial and urban development. Its use allows a form of active control over the excess of norms regulating the planning and design practice. Many of his studio's recent works may be considered datascapes in that they have sought to say something about the limitations that may be encountered, limitations that might be imposed by society, regulations, or the rules of the construction industry. 'Artistic' intuition acts within the use of technology, in the way we look at things, and like a sort of mirror, it reflects these constraints. Normally it is very difficult to reveal those restrictions because they are 'hidden' within other parameters. But when pushed to extremes these limitations come out, and then it is possible to analyse and discuss them.[6]

The timeframe that marks the beginning of the professional activity of MVRDV is a four-year period distinguished by a number of projects that are noteworthy for the singular, emphatically iconic way the respective programmes are translated into. The salient features of these works are their ability to bring into focus themes that are considered particularly 'urgent' by contemporary society (and particularly the Dutch), especially the one regarding 'congestion,' and to furnish effective, concrete, and even surprising responses to them, responses that are the fruit of a new and anti-dogmatic planning and design approach that is free of preconceptions.

The four projects listed below, albeit different in terms of constructive importance and effort, highlight constants that are also found in later works. The most relevant is the tendency of the object to address the dual dimension of architecture and urban planning. This is reflected in its configuration as a signal on a grand scale whose inner space is a rich 'labyrinthine' complex represented an expression of freedom and the overturning of any preconceived schemes.

[1] Luis Moreno Mansilla, Emilio Tuñon, 'The Space of Optimism. A Conversation with Winy Maas, Jacob van Rijs, and Natalie de Vries,' El Croquis, no. 86, 1997.
[2] Rem Koolhaas, Sedici anni di Oma, 1988, in Jacques Lucan, Oma. Rem Koolhaas. Architetture 1970-1990, Electa, Milan 1991, p. 162.
[3] Stan Allen's definition.
[4] Jos Bosman, Form Follows Fiction. From Meta-City to Mega-City, in Véronique Patteeuw (edited by), Reading MVRDV, NAi Publishers, Rotterdam 2003, p. 91.
[5] Stan Allen, 'Artificial ecologies: the work of MVRDV,' El Croquis, no. 86, 1997.
[6] Luis Moreno Mansilla, Emilio Tuñon, op. cit.

Berlin Voids

Berlin Voids in Berlin (1991), in addition to being MVRDV's first project, was also an occasion for the group to define a number of fundamental choices in a sort of ideal manifesto laying the groundwork for future developments. It is important to note that this proposal contains many of the theoretical and conceptual elements that constituted the substance of the 'turning point' in the 1990s. These were carried forward by the young Dutch generation and analysed, debated, and enriched via numerous conferences, exhibitions, books, and articles, giving rise to two currents: the need to achieve detachment from modernist ideology and its dogmas (one of which is standardisation); and the relationship with the notion of *density*, as laid out by Koolhaas in *Delirious New York*, whose epitome lies in the downtown athletic club, a turbulent superimposition of metropolitan life, a machine in which the very excesses of hedonism become redemption, a conventional or banal skyscraper while also the most extravagant programme of our century.[1] The complex designed by MVRDV reflects the idea of a *scission* between the outside and the inside, and of *congestion*, which is a key ingredient in any metropolitan architecture or plan.[2]

The distinction of Berlin Voids is thus its configuration along that intriguing, oxymoronic line that aims to unite two antithetical realities: on the one hand, the idea of *concentration* expressed by the macro-container with an external image akin to collective housing projects, the standardised dwelling unit; on the other, the application of the opposite principle of total *differentiation* of spaces within the residential block by means of the multitude of combinatory possibilities among the thirty-four for-

Longitudinal section
of car park

mal types that range from the 'folded house' to the 'cantilevered house,' from the 'cross house' to the 'zig-zag house,' and so on.

The area addressed in the design contest is in the Prenzlauerberg district, constituted by the characteristic block houses with inner courtyards (Mietskasernen) and situated along the borderline between the two Berlins at the site of a former checkpoint. The contest requested designs for a residential building with 284 apartments and 30,000 square metres of commercial space with the objective of carrying out an urban 'facelift' in the area.

MVRDV made the choice to steer away from traditional types and instead to pursue an assonance with the Grosshäusen seen in the distance. They designed an imposing volume developing upwards whose intent is to stand as an image of 'progress' breaking away from tradition. It is a 'neighbourhood-building,' or a 'vertical neighbourhood,' whose complex and imposing structure recapitulates all the functions on both the architectural and the urban scale. The myriad combinatory possibilities among the residential types, with their intricate and surprising spatial solutions arranged like a puzzle inside a gigantic wrapper, are simply the counterpart of the inner dynamism of contemporary society, of the progressive intermixing of different social and cultural groups and different styles of life.

[1] Rem Koolhaas, *New York/La Villette*, *1985*, in Jacques Lucan, op. cit., p. 161.
[2] Rem Koolhaas, *Conversations with the students*, Rice School of Architecture and Princeton Architectural Press, Huston – New York 1996, p. 13.

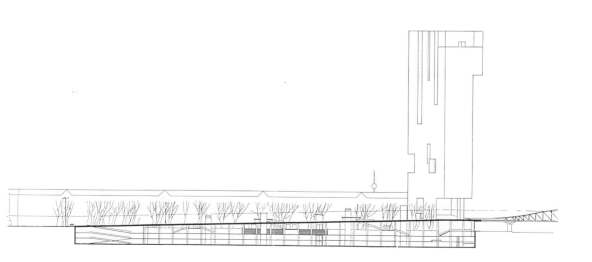

Partial section

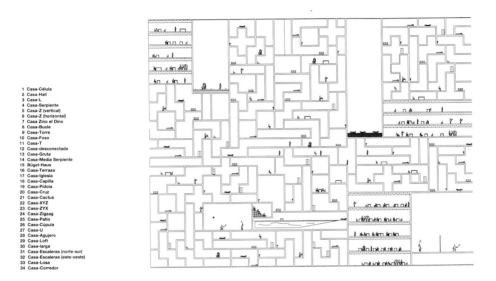

1 Casa-Célula
2 Casa-Hall
3 Casa-L
4 Casa-Serpiente
5 Casa-Z (vertical)
6 Casa-Z (horizontal)
7 Casa Zino el Dino
8 Casa-Bucle
9 Casa-Torre
10 Casa-Foso
11 Casa-T
12 Casa-desconectada
13 Casa-Gruta
14 Casa-Media Serpiente
15 Bügel-Haus
16 Casa-Terraza
17 Casa-Iglesia
18 Casa-Capilla
19 Casa-Pidola
20 Casa-Cruz
21 Casa-Cactus
22 Casa-XYZ
23 Casa-ZYX
24 Casa-Zigzag
25 Casa-Patio
26 Casa-Cúpula
27 Casa-U
28 Casa-Agujero
29 Casa-Loft
30 Casa-larga
31 Casa-Escaleras (norte-sur)
32 Casa-Escaleras (este-oeste)
33 Casa-Losa
34 Casa-Corredor

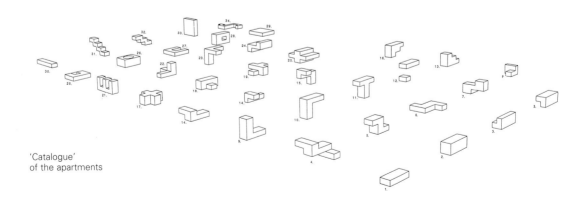

'Catalogue'
of the apartments

Open-Air Theatre

Open-Air Theatre in Delft (1992) is MVRDV's first realised work. It is a multipurpose piece of equipment equipped as a basketball court (with grandstand for twelve to sixteen year-olds) and open-air theatre. The construction responds to the variegated set of needs of a group of schools belonging to a small local community. MVRDV sought to give an original interpretation to the project, proposing an object with a strong iconic character resembling a chair by Charles Eames but on a gargantuan scale[1] that serves as a common area and community gathering place. As such, it is configured as a signal, and one that is quite easily distinguished against the flat Dutch landscape. It is a 'scenic dike,' an arrival point for bike paths and winding footpaths. And in spite of its modest dimensions, in the image it seems to echo the same totalising spirit that characterises MVRDV's previous project.

The construction method for the 'seashell' form is quite interesting. It was built using an experimental technique that Maas had used earlier during his internship at OMA, involving four layers of reinforced concrete in a sort of plywood-like structure. This method allows maximum plasticity of form and strength with a minimal thickness (only 16 cm).

[1] Kathy Battista, Florian Migsch, *The Netherlands*, Könemann – Ellipsis, London – Cologne 1998, p. 316.

Church

In the concept of its spatial layout, the *Church* in Barendrecht (1993) develops the hypothesis of a convergence between the classical approach to faith and the trend towards renewal ushered in with the Vatican II Council.

The initial idea was for a low, windowless structure with a rectangular footprint termed by its designers as being 'enclosed like a rock in a sea of two-story houses.' It is a horizontal monolith standing over a large pool on a series of pillars, creating the perceptual effect of a 'floating object.' The design of the foundational floor allows the light reflected off the water to penetrate into the sanctuary. It also serves the functional purposes of accommodating bicycle parking, the vestibule, the recreation room, the child-care centre, the kitchen, the sanitary facilities, the storeroom, and the utility room.

The church floor is not completely horizontal, but slightly 'creased' or 'folded' in a number of places along different lines. Taken together, these contours produce, as the designers put it, the sensation of a 'mountainous landscape.' It is a sort of artificial ecology composed of planes with different forms and slopes, which in conditioning the arrangement of the fixtures (the long wood and steel balconies) orients the gaze of the faithful towards specific objectives inside the church.

The floor is covered with a composite of silicon and crushed stone and is interpreted as a floating plane.

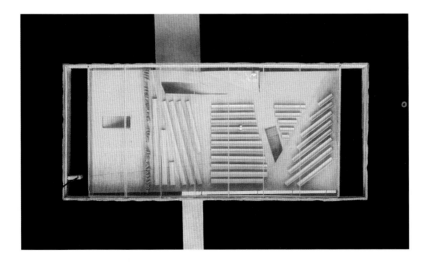

Top view of model

Front view of model
with plans, elevations,
and sections

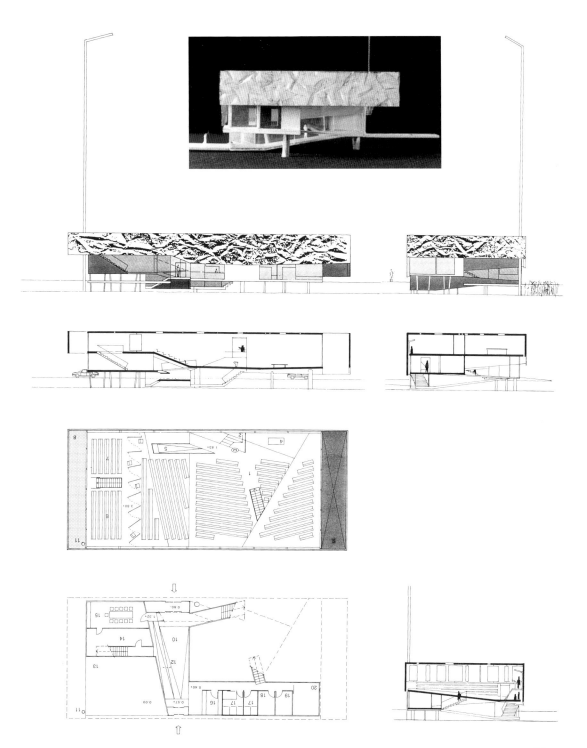

23

View of model

Axonometry

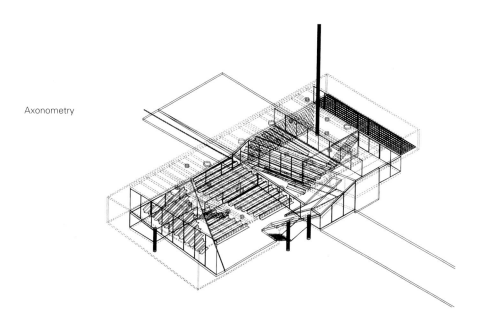

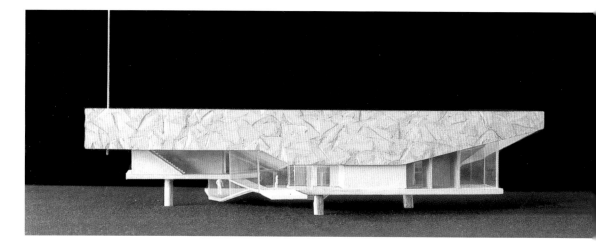

Sloterpark Swimming-Pool

Sloterpark Swimming Pool in Amsterdam (1994) was the object of a project to expand a pool originally built in the 1950s. The architects proposed to place the new pools above the existing one, thus creating a compact, layered structure. The intention was to leave intact the surrounding area with its trees and to create a volume with a strong identity and an internal spatial complexity, all based on the clearly manifested idea of overall spatial continuity.

The special character of the interior, achieved by 'folding' the vertical and horizontal planes, reproposes the same design solution as in the Barendrecht church and in the contemporary plans for the Meent Department Store Building in Binnenrotte (1994).

MVRDV's intention was to foster the coexistence of two ideologically different types of recreational structures (which also stand for two different phases in the country's history): the large old pool with its Spartan design for intensive use by the general public; and the newly conceived small pools that express a more intimate character and a more refined lifestyle.

The existing pool was covered using a gridwork of beams with a thickness equal to that of the floor. The folds in the walkways both distinguish and unite, through a continuity of traffic flow, the different activity zones. One thus moves from the sauna area to a gallery with a rock-climbing wall looking onto the diving pool. Or else from a pool with a gently sloping bottom one goes through a 'saddle' to reach the somewhat separated lower zone with a gallery looking onto the squash courts and the fenced-in area with the sports equipment. The roof is grassed and supports foot traffic. A last fold on its surface creates a small 'beach': a secluded rest spot with a view of the Sloterpark.

Structure set into the landscape

Views of model

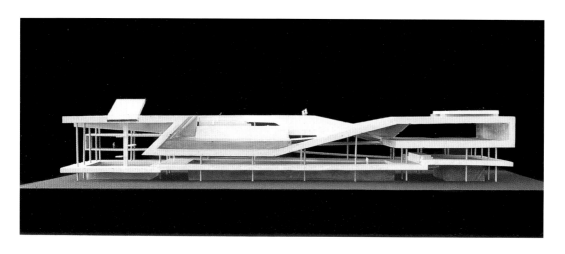

The First Important Works

MVRDV's second quadrennium is distinguished by a series of projects imbued with a strongly innovative spirit and a provocative and intellectually stimulating charge that would soon make the work of MVRDV known to a general audience, partially thanks to a skillful use of communication tools.

The works in this period are characterised by their direct goal of being built, for their immediate reckoning with reality, and for the incorporation of the method of 'negotiation' into the design process, a modus operandi with deep roots in Holland. As Lootsma comments, the orientation of the Dutch social state over the past century is probably the most characteristic example of this traditional form of democracy based on negotiation and a strong faith in planning. In this regard, MVRDV's most incisive contribution to the contemporary architectural debate has been that of establishing a method for considering architecture, urban design, and planning as a continuous field in which different points of view may be brought to bear on different levels, in different contexts, and on different scales. The realm may be analytical and programmatic, or visionary and utopian, but the process always involves full respect for communication and collaboration with the other parties involved whether they be political or private organisations.[1]

The OMA studio has developed its own original method of applying this praxis in the conviction that the reality organised by architecture and urban planning has to be quantifiable, i.e., reducible to numerical terms and thus translatable into graphs and statistical tables. MVRDV's great merit has been its ability to refine that procedure, introducing a process of negotiation that generates much of the project itself. While the group's works demonstrate a certain attention to the linguistic-architectonic universe, the formal aspect is not the main objective. Much of the design schemes are left open-ended to allow the users to make suggestions and to incorporate different aesthetic sensibilities.

In March 1997, near the end of this cycle, MVRDV's participation in the exhibition *Nine + One. Ten Young Dutch Architectural Offices* provided an excellent opportunity for drawing up the first 'balance sheet' of their theoretical path. As the name suggests, the important cultural event involved ten design groups selected by Kristin Feireiss[2], who at the time was the director of NAi (Netherlands Architectural Institute) of Rotterdam, and was organised as a series of independent exhibitions. The initiative reviewed the research being done by the young Dutch architects and represented an important occasion for comparing and sharing ideas and exploring the most interesting projects of newly emerging studios.

Villa VPRO, Hilversum
1993–97. Night view

29

The '+ One' in the title stood to indicate the independent spirit of the various protagonists as written on the inside cover of the catalogue: 'There is always one, although never the same, who disagrees with the others.' The event highlighted the lack of a shared analytical methodology in the approach to programmatic and spatial issues. Hence the architectural image had become the result of a strategy of investigation rather than an aesthetic goal.

MVRDV presented a series of projects for the occasion that gave an incisive albeit partial overview of their work: Sloterpark Swimming-Pool, Three Porters' Lodges, WoZoCo's, and Villa VPRO. Their blurb in the catalogue explained that in the space of six years the studio had grown to its current size of thirteen architects with multidisciplinary backgrounds giving them broad perspectives in various sectors. It also stated that their apparent lack of consideration for the traditional boundaries between architecture, urban design, interior design, and product design was not a simple option, but a basic principle.[3]

[1] Bart Lootsma, *What is (really) to be done?*, in Véronique Patteeuw (edited by), op. cit., p. 25.
[2] The others present along with MVRDV were Bosch Haslett, Marx & Steketee, Maxwan, NL Architects, NOX, Buro Schie, Endry van Velzen, VMX Architects, and René van Zuuk.
[3] Marijke Kuper (edited by), *Nine + One. Ten Young Dutch Architectural Offices*, NAi Publishers, Rotterdam 1997, p. 57.

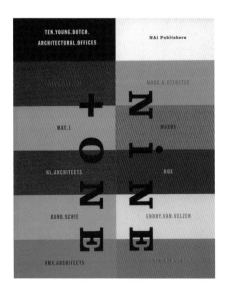

Three Porters' Lodges, Hoge Veluwe National Park

Three Porters' Lodges, Hoge Veluwe National Park (1994–95) are three pavilions located at the Arnhem, Hoenderloo, and Otterlo entrances to the extensive Hoge Veluwe landscape reserve. The park is famous for its natural beauty and for a number of important architectural works including the St. Hubertus hunting lodge of Hendrik Petrus Berlage (1916) and the Kröller-Müller museum designed in various stages by Henry van de Velde (1938–53) and expanded in the 1970s by Wim G. Quist.

The MVRDV pavilions are small service structures for park visitors. Their singular appearance is the result of a 'deformation' of the archetypical form of a house in response to specific environmental constraints such as the position of the pavilion in relation to a well-trafficked road, to a bicycle parking area, or to a nearby tree. Each pavilion has its own particular layout and facing materials: wood for the one in Arnhem, Corten steel and bricks for those at Hoenderloo and Otterlo. The entire volume of each pavilion is finished in these materials, including the roof, the doors, and the hatch-awnings that open above the large windows. When closed, the small buildings become strange and mysterious objects. Their singular forms must not, nevertheless, distract attention from the essence of the design concept embodied in their construction. Their three-dimensional form emerges from the surface of a sheet of paper on which the different sides are drawn; as in certain children's games, by folding the sheet according to directions, the object takes form. This would categorise the design concept as a variant on folding architecture, a theme that has already been broadly explored, albeit in different ways, in previous works and—as we will see— also in others to follow.

Arnhem. The wooden pavilion

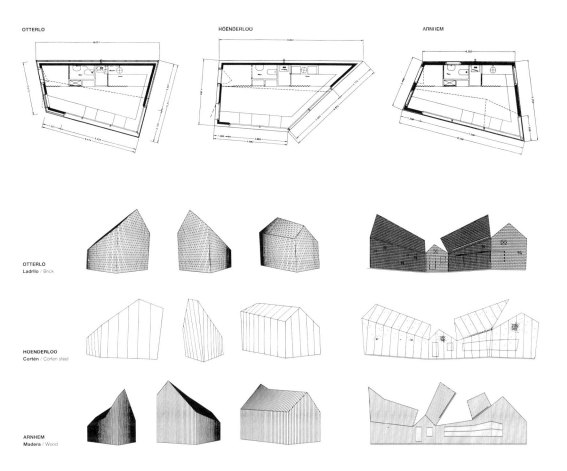

OTTERLO

HOENDERLOO

ARNHEM

OTTERLO
Ladrllo / Brick

HOENDERLOO
Cortén / Corten steel

ARNHEM
Madera / Wood

Plans and volumes
of the three pavilions

Hoenderloo. The Corten
steel pavilion

WoZoCo's Apartments for Elderly People

WoZoCo's Apartments for Elderly People in Amsterdam-Osdorp (1994–97) is a residential complex for people over fifty-five years old. It is positioned on the north-south axis of the Osdorp neighbourhood, a development from the 1950s and 1960s based on an urban plan designed by Cornelius van Eesteren.

The goal was to construct a building for hundred families on a given footprint that could only accommodate eighty-seven without depriving the surrounding buildings of their legislated share of sun exposure. Adding an extension would have meant occupying green areas in a zone where natural assets were to be protected. It was not possible to increase the depth of the building since it would have altered the size of the lodgings. The solution to the problem was to take advantage of a regulation that forbade direct northern exposure for the apartments. This, along with the application of sophisticated technology, would lead to the idea to cantilever the thirteen remaining units onto the wall with the external walkways, facing towards the polder and along the east-west axis. This daring design was achieved using a grid of steel beams that were coated to protect them from fire and to soundproof them.

Each cantilevered volume has its own distinctive character thanks to variations in window positions, balcony sizes, colours, and materials.

View of the south wall

Plans, elevations, and sections

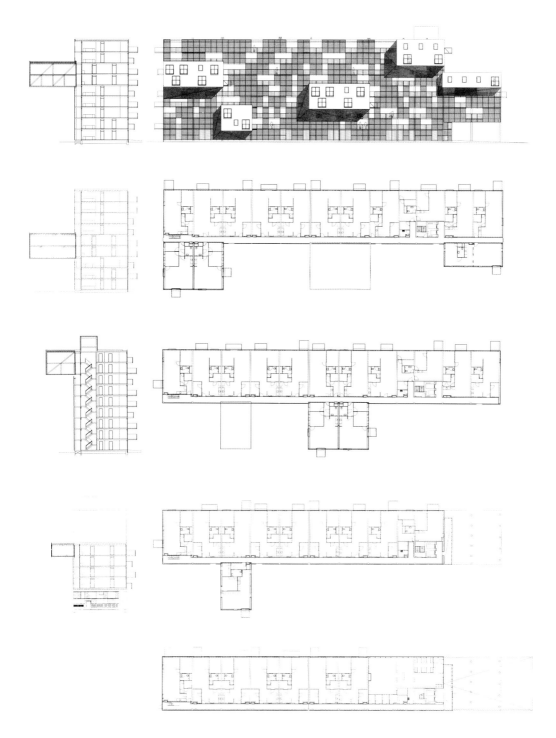

View of the south wall
and detail of the north
façade

View of the north and east
façades

Villa VPRO

Villa VPRO, Hilversum (1994–97) houses a public television broadcaster and, as the designers state, it is a hybrid between a villa and an office. The name given to he work indicates the desire to maintain a close conceptual and organisational relationship between the thirteen small villas previously occupied by the company and the most recent structure designed by MVRDV.

The salient characteristic of the original arrangement was the significant degree of autonomy and close contacts between producers and programmers, albeit with clear limits in keeping with rational organisation of work. However, given the excellent quality standards achieved by the network, it was felt to be important that the same characteristics of freedom and personal independence that had previously characterised and stimulated the broadcaster's operating method were transferred into this new building.

The area chosen for the construction is near a small lake surrounded by woods and moors. Considering the severe height constraints imposed by local zoning regulations, the adopted solution was a very compact five-storey building which hugged the ground contours in order to reduce its impact on the surrounding environment. The structure thus seeks to present itself as an 'element' of the landscape with which it seeks continuity. The vegetation that was removed from the building plot was replaced by a green roof under which a 'geological formation' developed, composed of a series of floors.[1]

The arrangement of the interior space goes against all traditional schemes. It is conceived as an open space, with the addition of absolutely original solutions. The traffic areas are full of rises, ramps, stairs, and galleries. The ceilings are at different heights. The various rooms differ as to their spatial configurations. The work areas in the central part of the building are illuminated via skylights and small patios.

The project reflects the development of the idea elaborated for Europan 2 in Berlin. Regarding that original project, Aaron Betsky pointed out that the myriad possible combinations of the dwelling units guided them to propose a sort of puzzle composed of stepped interiors that intersect to

Overall view

create a compact, habitable environment with infinite possibilities for transformation. This was the strategy they later applied to the Villa VPRO project, which was a sort of 'hungry box' that engulfed elements of different projects into a single rectangular volume. In combination, these two approaches produced buildings without beginning or end, without hierarchy, and without distinct ambits. The conceptual act of uniting all the elements of the programme, the arrangement of these parts as closely and as distinctly as possible, and the creation of a structure with the smallest number of elements for accommodating these pieces has become the official trademark of their work.[2]

From every point in the interior it is possible to maintain visual contact with the outside. The glass walls can be opened to provide an even more direct relationship with the environment.

The building façade, as in Koolhaas's Educatorium, presents itself conceptually as a 'cut surface,' a section of the construction sliced at an apparently random point to show the inner space with no interposed structure to safeguard privacy. The architects point out that exposing the interior is a very current design method and that while it might seem a bit perverse, it resembles in some ways the contemporary intermixture of public and private: you cross the street on the zebra stripes and hear a neighbour's amorous conversation on the telephone with his girlfriend, every day people shed their privacy on television to make a spectacle of themselves. The timeworn boundaries between public and private seem to have become completely irrelevant.[3]

[1] MVRDV, *The landscape is the building*, in Jaime Salazar (edited by), *MVRDV at VPRO*, Actar, Barcelona 1998, p. 64.
[2] Aaron Betsky, *MVRDV: The Matrix Pro-ject*, in Véronique Patteeuw (edited by), op. cit., p. 19.
[3] Luis Moreno Mansilla, Emilio Tuñon, op. cit.

Configuration diagrams

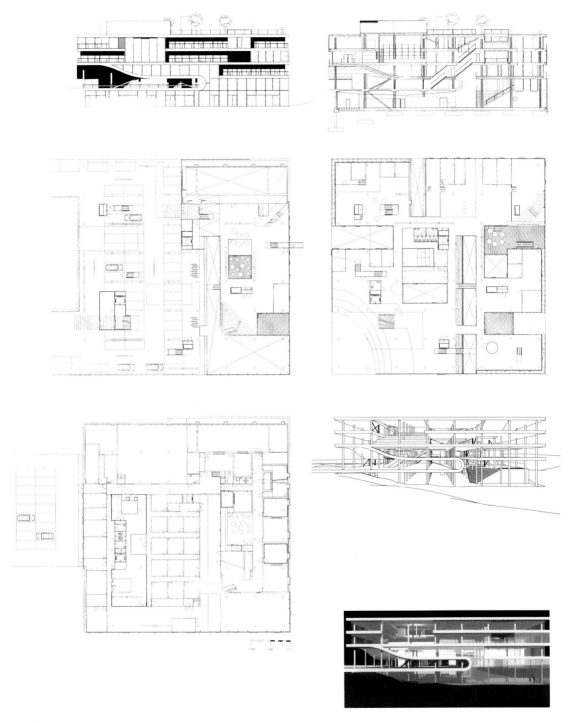

Plans, elevations,
and sections

External view of building

Interior view

RVU Building

The *RVU Building* in Hilversum (1994–97) is located in the same area as Villa VPRO (and other television networks such as VARA and NPS). The strong landscape constraints spurred the architects in this case as well to create a building that integrates well into its natural setting.

The building is a sort of long horizontal prism positioned in such a way as to take advantage of the gentle slope of the ground so that one end of it is hidden (almost 'driven into' the ground) while the rest rises up on delicate steel pillars as the ground slopes away from it. This space thus delimited provides access to the building. It is arranged simply with a parking area for bicycles on one side and a group of lava fragments on the other that delimit the walkway up to the entrance. The entrance is in the middle of the building halfway up the stairs leading to the roof. The grassed roof is an extension of the adjacent land surface, and accessible to the public via a stairway that cuts across the centre of the building.

The interior is arranged so as to offer an unbroken but partitionable workspace. Here it is divided into three zones, each with specific characteristics corresponding to the needs of those working there. Hence we see one area set up as a freely arranged work unit, another with two corridors (and the stairway in the middle) flanked by offices, and the third with a central passageway providing access to differently sized offices and leading to the company canteen. This area corresponds to the cantilevered part of the building and has a full glass wall looking out over the campus. The rest of the building has narrow openings like slits in correspondence to the work areas. It is faced in Corten sheet steel.

View of the roof

Structure set into
the landscape

Plan and exploded
axonometric view
of the building

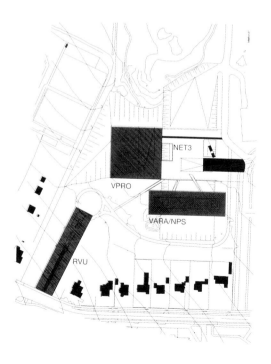

NET3

VPRO

VARA/NPS

RVU

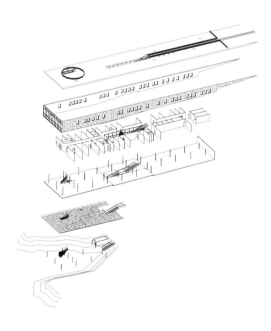

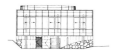

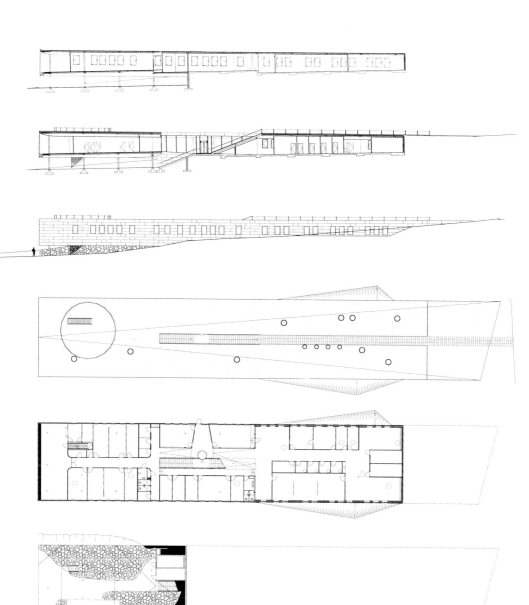

Double House

Double House in Utrecht (1995–97) is a dual-family dwelling located on the Koningslaan, a broad suburban street, across from the Wilhelminpark, a large 19th century park.

MVRDV's method of 'negotiation' with the client was extended in this case to de architectengroep (represented by Bjarne Mastenbroek), the Utrecht studio with whom they would work to develop the project.

Having discarded the overly predictable option of separating the two properties with a vertical wall, the designers carried out a more subtle process of 'negotiation' between the two neighbours. The discussion of the often contrasting needs of the two families ended up enriching the quality of the respective dwellings beyond what had initially been imagined.

The desire to occupy as small a footprint as possible in order to leave a small space for a garden behind the house led the architects to reduce its depth and extend it upwards (four to five floors).

Externally the building is a simple prism that reveals nothing of the internal complexity of the two apartments, which differ greatly in size and spatial arrangement.

The view towards the park, the independent accesses to the street, the garden, and the rooftop terrace are some of the needs shared by both clients.

The smaller apartment has a front door that leads directly into a large ground floor room with a wall that opens onto the internal garden. This area has a kitchenette in the corner and a stairway leading directly to the second floor sitting room (it bypasses the first floor). There are two bedrooms on the floor above. On the top floor there is a small bathroom with a terrace.

The larger apartment has a garage 'dug into' the building volume on the ground floor next to the entry. Inside the apartment there is a guest room and a stairway leading to the first floor with a large salon and the kitchen. On the second floor there are two bedrooms. On the third floor there are two more bedrooms and a bath, and a studio with a spiral staircase leading to the rooftop terrace through an openable skylight.

This work is distinguished by the mutual presence of two contrasting aspects: the geometrical purity of the volume and the extreme freedom with which the internal spaces find a capacity to shape themselves in perfect harmony with the needs of the inhabitants. The exuberant dynamism of the interior is reflected in the two main sides of the prism only via the zig-zag pattern of openings in the dark surface of the rust-coloured Betonplex panels used to face the structure, giving them a sort of sombre lightness and an austere and penetrating formal style.

Urban setting for the
building

Development of the design
concept

| 161094
2 STOREYS 14M DEEP | 231194
4 STOREYS 7 METER DEEP | 141294
HOUSE IN A HOUSE | 231295
ALTERNATING FLOORS 1 | 040195
ALTERNATING FLOORS 2 | 120195
ALTERNATING FLOORS 3 | 200295
ALTERNATING FLOORS 4 | 090395
OUTDOOR SPACE | 130495
FINAL RESULT |

View of the project

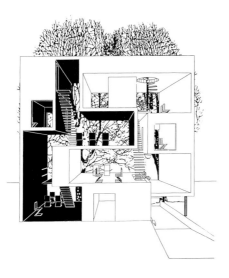

Elevation section

Elevation, sections,
and floor plans

Detail of the wall facing
the road

One of the special features of MVRDV's work is that it develops within an ideal 'intermediate zone' composed of superimpositions and subtle interchanges between the conceptual and the real. As the architects put it, if there had been no *Farmax* there would have been no WoZoCo's, at least not as we know it; without *3D City*, there would have been no Pinault; without Silodam, no *Functionmixer* ... Even the small scale projects have the qualities to give information and tools applicable to broader scenarios.[1]

The architects found occasion within this zone to establish fruitful interactions. On the one hand they came into it with a strong ideological and cultural thrust supported by statistical analysis, and on the other they expressed a noteworthy creative potential intent on fostering large-scale involvement. The two books, *Farmax* and *Metacity/Datatown* (the first of a long series of writings), represent a clear indication of the choice of operational method that distinguishes their pathway of exploration.

As Betsky observes, they are part of Generation 1.0, they are architects involved in goal-oriented design. Heirs of a century of attempts to define the discipline within an increasingly abstract and data-guided culture, they have chosen a particular alternative to engineering, organisation, and research-oriented systems. Their projects aim at transforming abstract statistical information into concrete forms.[2]

Farmax, begun in 1994[3] and completed in 1998, was their first theoretical text. The volume presents a series of articles and MVRDV projects, many of which were carried out with the collaboration of students from the Delft University of Technology, the Berlage Institute of Amsterdam[4], and the Academy of Architecture and Urban Planning of Rotterdam, together with a number of other designers. It also contains scientific, statistical, and socio-anthropological writings by scholars from different disciplines. The common thread running through the work and uniting its heterogeneous elements is the theme of *density*, as seen in the book's subtitle *Excursions on Density*. In the opening piece, *Greyness on the Dutch Mesa*, we read that vast areas of the Netherlands are invaded by a 'material' composed of low-cost houses with gardens, low-rent offices, warehouses, farm-style factories, areas for motocross, and other low density structures. The authors ask the question of how society is to cope with this urban 'material' that is not wholly appraisable. They warn that if this condition is accepted and the present trend continues unchecked, most of the still undeveloped areas will be covered, and Dutch society will be immersed in a general 'greyness'. They then set out to explore the theme of whether it might be possible to rework this fabric by

Left
Illustration from *Farmax*

raising density to an extreme and breaking up the pattern with insertions or polarities.[5] The book examines the potentials of these extremes without ignoring their negative aspects. It presents the world of the 'extreme Floor Area Ratio', hence FAR MAX.

What the authors seek to highlight in their hefty volume are the results of their thinking on the development of the counterposition between the building and the landscape, examining possibilities for reorganising or reinventing that relationship. On the one hand the architectural object tends to present itself as an ideal extension of the landscape. On the other, it aims to merge into a new and more complex structure that incorporates it (as is the case with the Dutch Pavilion at Expo 2000 in Hannover).

In *Farmax*, MVRDV's examination of the theme of density reflects their approach to design as is so well expressed in the motto 'research replaces imagination' and which originates in a series of thoughts and questions they have posited regarding certain fundamental current design issues. As Winy Maas sees it, everything is doable, we can imagine any object, nothing seems strange or extravagant anymore. He wonders what we can do in such circumstances. Should we aim for the ultimate extravagance? Are we perhaps suffering from the 'effete object', the consequence of the multitude of objects that seek to capture our attention, all shouting to tell us something? In our search for the 'extraordinary' within the 'unique', the expression of the single object has become ridiculous. In a 'sea of uniqueness', the single object simply ceases to exist.[6] These are all questions that seek to relieve the architects of the onerous responsibility of 'acting as society's godfathers' and to shift architecture directly into the era of doubt and relativism. The consequence is that artistic intuition is replaced by 'research'.[7]

The particular meaning they attribute to the term *research* is a key element in understanding their concept of design, something became increasingly clear with their ongoing production of works. In each one of them the architects start with a minute investigation of the facts, i.e., laws, regulations, conditions, experiences, available financing, client needs, and a host of other things. This data set is then translated into diagrams which are superimposed upon one another to create the framework which will constrain the design hypotheses. Oftentimes the margins of freedom, of concrete operational possibility, are surprisingly broader. This method is dubbed *datascape*, where form becomes the result of an extrapolation or hypothesis of a broader data set of demands.[8] Once the *research* path is completed, the materials undergo a process of transformation.

Expanding this theme, which represents the focal point of their design methodology, in 1999 MVRDV published the book *Metacity/Datatown*.[9] The new text examines the consequences of globalisation and, in particular, of the general expansion of urbanisation. The authors state that the systematic reduction of free areas resulting from this urban growth compromises the chances of preserving a proper balance of natural resources that are vital for our survival. The previously undeveloped parts are colonised and become zones of concentrated urbanisation. Nature is thus transformed into a crowded place and agriculture, which has to be intensified to meet rising demand, is left with less and less available space.[10]

It is a degenerative developmental process that affects the entire planet, and its dimension has rendered traditional instruments inadequate for grasping the real scale of the event and controlling it. In response, the authors propose statistical investigation as part of a possible methodology of intervention. As Maas observes, while data selected and correlated according to selected criteria and hypotheses provide the illusion of reality and verity, numbers actually have no meaning if unaccompanied by human intuition; a number free of all influences, free from interpretation, is inconceivable.[11]

The implementation of numerically-supported 'extreme scenarios' allows MVRDV to prefigure, evaluate, and elaborate possible future situations. *Metacity* is thus not a project, but a prelude to further explorations that might inspire much needed self-examination in the worlds of architecture and urban design, and even a redefinition of the profession.[12]

In this approach to reality, Betsky sees a singular analogy with the film *Matrix* (which also came out in 1998), where at the end we see a world that dissolves into a downpour of data. He feels that while *Matrix* may merely be a paranoiac commercial Hollywood science fiction film, MVRDV works with that very same shower of data. But since reality is not a film

Illustration from *Farmax*

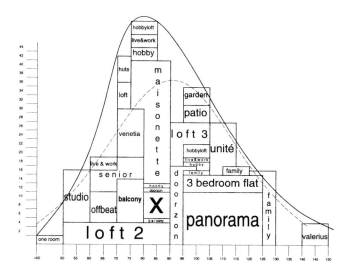

and they are architects, their job is to give form to all those zeroes and ones. As designers they accept the fact that our reality can only be nothing more than the exterior appearance of information and then set themselves to the task of bringing the lessons learned in architecture to bear on this particular condition. He sees the flood of data as a sort of delicious swirling bubble bath in which we can also immerse ourselves.[13]

Datatown is the application of that conceptual and programmatic mindset to a given sample of area: a city described exclusively by information, based on data, a Metacity without topography, without a definite ideology, representation, or context.

We may start from the 'dimensional' value, one of the data that has historically been an important element in defining a city's identity. If in the Middle Ages it was equal to four kilometres travelled on foot and in the 1920s it was twenty kilometres travelled by bicycle, with the advent of high speed trains, that distance now is on the order of four hundred kilometres. On this basis, MVRDV determined that Datatown is a city four hundred kilometres square with a population density four times that of Holland. It is the densest place on Earth. It is a city for 241 million inhabitants, the entire USA in one city.[14] But Datatown is also autarkic and its problems have to be resolved within its own confines. The issue of its survival will regard six fundamental parameters: residence, agriculture, forests, energy, waste, water.

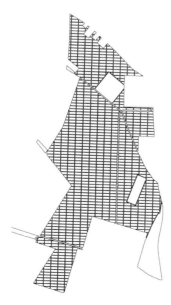

Illustration from *Farmax*

[1] Cristina Díaz Moreno, Efrén García Grinda, 'Redefining the Tools of Radicalism. Interview with MVRDV', in *El Croquis*, no. 111, 2002.

[2] Aaron Betsky, op. cit., p. 17.

[3] On the crest of a wave of interest generated by a 1993 OMA study presented at the *Air Alexander Design Festival* consisting of a proposal for the 'total Dutch city' with green parkland in its centre and a population density similar to that of Manhattan or Los Angeles.

[4] Originally in Amsterdam, the Berlage Institute later moved to Rotterdam.

[5] Richard Koek, Winy Maas, Jacob van Rijs, *Greyness on the Dutch Mesa*, in MVRDV, *Farmax. Excursions on Density*, 010 Publishers, Rotterdam 1998, pp. 19–23.

[6] Winy Maas, *Datascape*, in MVRDV, *Farmax...* op. cit., p. 100.

[7] Ibidem, p. 103

[8] Ibidem, p. 103.

[9] MVRDV, *Metacity/Datatown*, 010 Publishers, Rotterdam 1999; the book grew out of an idea of Winy Maas and was created by MVRDV. It represents a development on the video installation of the same name in the Aedes East gallery in Berlin in March 1999.

[10] Ibidem, p. 16.

[11] Ibidem, p. 198.

[12] Ibidem, p. 19.

[13] Aaron Betsky, op. cit., p. 11.

[14] MVRDV, *Metacity/Datatown* op. cit., p. 59.

Illustration from *Farmax*

New Projects

MVRDV's third quadrennium brought forth a series of interesting and realised works, some of which had begun to be developed in previous years.

The central theme around which they rotate is that of *density* (a strongly felt issue in highly populated Holland), which MVRDV addresses in its own special way through a multidisciplinary investigation based on a layered study embracing many aspects of reality. The issue of the lack of space is the same one experienced in even more dramatic forms in urban areas in the East and West centred around Tokyo, Singapore, Hong Kong, or New York.

For MVRDV, this theme—beyond its natural anthropological, sociological, economic, and political implications—represents a serious form of deprivation of personal liberty and a sort of violence directed at the subjective sphere. It results in the denial of a fundamental physical and mental need for daily well-being. It means depriving people of a fundamental faculty of choice and interfering with their freedom to manage their own vital sphere, which includes the ability to move physically—the most spontaneous and immediate expression of occupying (and dominating) a space.

Dutch Pavilion, Hannover
1997–2000. Elevation detail

Two Houses

Two Houses in Borneo-Sporenburg, Amsterdam (1996–2000), are two houses in the new, elegant Borneo-Sporenburg neighbourhood, not far from
Amsterdam's historic centre and whose masterplan was developed by West
8. In this project MVRDV does not miss the opportunity to couple this theme
with that of *congestion*, enriching the dual and circumscribed project with
interesting design stimuli.

The houses are built on two long and narrow lots (Parcel 12 measures
5 x 16 metres; Parcel 18 measures 4.2 x 16 metres). The method used in
the West 8 plan, where the urbanised territory of the island is cut into swaths,
is reproposed on the narrow strips of land allotted to each of the 9.5-me-
tre-high houses. On one side the houses face onto the street, on the other they face the canal.

The designers' intention was to transform the disadvantageous anom-
alous shapes of the two footprints and the meagre spatial capacity into a
chance for formal enrichment, seeking to maximise the spaciousness and
versatility of the structures. To achieve this, they incorporated articulated
volumes (corresponding to specific rooms) and floors in an apparently free-
form fashion into the internal void of the two 'container-buildings'. Their
objective in doing so was to create, via columns of light from skylights,
prospects, floor elevation variations, and diversified spatial arrangements.
The evenly distributed natural lighting renders the spatial configuration
of the interiors 'transparent' so that they seem to expand outwards and
thereby make the dwellings feel larger.

View of the two projects
along the canal

Interior of Parcels 12
and 18

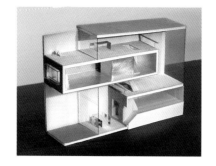 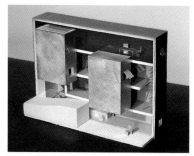

Plans, sections,
and elevations of Parcel 18

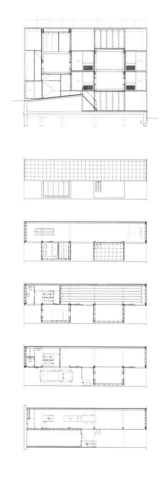 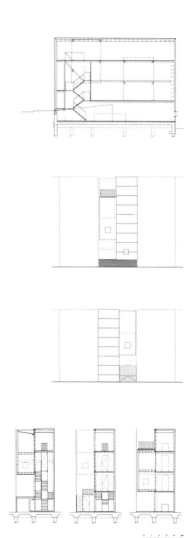

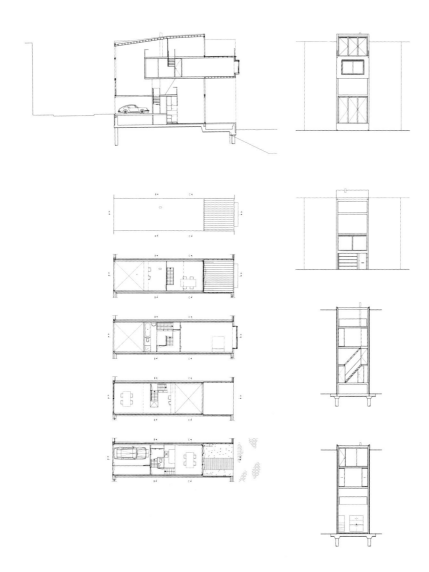

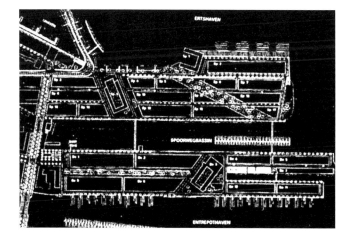

General plan

Dutch Pavilion

The *Dutch Pavilion* for the Hannover Expo 2000 (1997–2000) represents a possible response by Holland to the urgency of the ecological theme. For MVRDV it also constitutes the physical image of a series of theoretical hypotheses developed in previous years (collected in *Farmax*) on the theme of *density*.

The pavilion explores the theme of the relationship between artificial and natural and is surprising for its overall magical capacity to convey both complexity and risk. Perhaps more than any other work, the Dutch Pavilion, in the immediacy and incisiveness of its iconic message, is the Dutch culture's architectural statement before an international audience on issues relating to urban growth.

The work is not merely a celebration of how Holland 'creates space' but is also an indication of the importance of landscape architecture, one of the more important issues in the recent debate. The pavilion is an intelligent reworking of a type invented by OMA in the 1980s that never found concrete application. The combination of a medley of programmes and building types to be worked into the landscape has been one of the icons in Dutch architecture and territorial planning.[1]

The project develops the theme of reconciliation between technology and nature, developing further the notion of 'artificiality' as an epitome for the Dutch landscape, which has been completely redesigned by the constant work of humans. The structure presents an overlayering of six ways of occupying the landscape: the 'dune landscape' on the ground floor where the entrance and the information point are located; the 'greenhouse landscape', showing how the agricultural industry can contribute to the development of the technology-nature theme; the 'pot landscape', where a number of large pots for the plants upstairs and other hanging ones that contain video screens create a sinuous space composed of visual messages, images, lights, and colours; the 'forest landscape' composed of thick vegetation embellished with enormous tree trunks; the 'rain landscape' with an audiovisual theatre surrounded by a wall of water that functions as a screen; and the grass-covered 'polder landscape' on the roof with its modern windmills and a floating 'VIP island'.

[1] Anne Hoogewoning, Roemer van Toorn, Piet Vollaard, Arthur Wortmann (edited by), *Architecture in the Netherlands*, Nai Publishers, Rotterdam 2001, p. 145.

Overall view

Internal space organisation
diagram

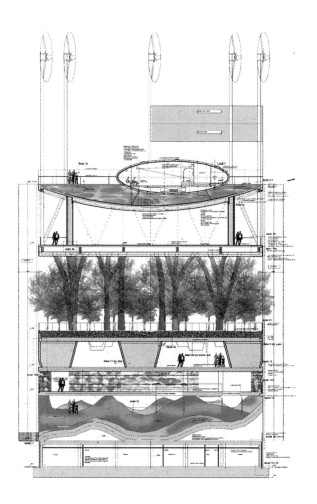

Technical and functional
diagrams

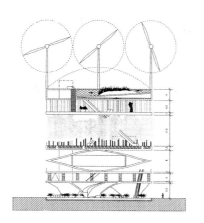

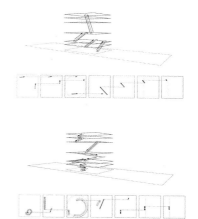

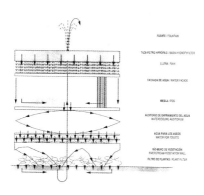

FUENTE / FOUNTAIN

TAZA-FILTRO HIDRÓFILO / BASIN-HYDROFYILTER

LLUVIA / RAIN

FACHADA DE AGUA / WATER FACADE

NIEBLA / FOG

AUDITORIO DE ENFRIAMIENTO DEL AGUA
WATERCOOLING AUDITORIUM

AGUA PARA LOS ASEOS
WATER FOR TOILETS

RÍO-MURO DE VEGETACIÓN / RIVERSTREAM VEGETATION WALL
FILTRO DE PLANTAS / PLANT FILTER

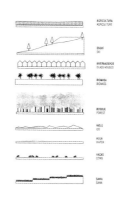

AGRICULTURA
AGRICULTURE

ESQUÍ
SKI

INVERNADEROS
GLASS HOUSES

BIOMASA
BIOMASS

BOSQUE
FOREST

HIELO
ICE

AGUA
WATER

VACAS
COWS

SAUNA
SANA

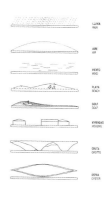

LLUVIA
RAIN

AIRE
AIR

VIENTO
WIND

PLAYA
BEACH

GOLF
GOLF

VIVIENDAS
HOUSING

GRUTA
GROTTO

OSTRA
OYSTER

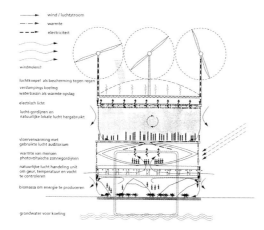

wind / luchtstroom
warmte
electriciteit

windmolens?

luchtkoepel als bescherming tegen regen
verdampings koeling
waterbassin als warmte opslag

electrisch licht

lucht-gordijnen en
natuurlijke lokale lucht hergebruikt

vloerverwarming met
gebrukte lucht auditorium

warmte van mensen
photovoltaische zonnegordijnen

natuurlijke lucht handeling unit
om geur, temperatuur en vocht
te controleren

biomassa om energie te produceren

grondwater voor koeling

	Calor Heat	Energía Energy	
			VIENTO-AIRE / WIND-AIR
			CALOR / HEAT
			ELECTRICIDAD / ELECTRICITY
		+	MOLINOS DE VIENTO / WINDMILLS
			CÚPULA DE AIRE QUE PROTEGE DE LA LLUVIA / AIR DOME FOR PROTECTION AGAINST RAIN ENFRIAMIENTO VAPOR / VAPOR COOLING TAZA DE ACUMULACIÓN DE CALOR / WATERBASIN AS HEATSTORAGE
	+	-	LUZ ELÉCTRICA / ELECTRICAL LIGHT
	+	-	CORTINA DE AIRE Y RECICLAJE DE AIRE INFERIOR AIR CURTAIN AND RE-USE NATURAL LOCAL AIR
			CALENTAMIENTO DEL SUELO CON AIRE RECICLADO DEL AUDITORIO FLOORHEATING WITH USED AIR OF AUSITORIUM
		+	CALOR HUMANO-CORTINA SOLAR FOTOVOLTAICA HEAT OF PEOPLE-PHOTOVOLTAIC SUN-CURTAIN
	+	-	ACONDICIONAMIENTO DE AIRE NATURAL PARA CONTROL DE OLORES, TEMPERATURA Y HUMEDAD / NATURAL AIR CONDITIONING TO CONTROL SMELL, TEMPERATURE AND MOIST
	+/-	+	BIOMASA PRODUCTORA DE ENERGÍA / BIOMASS TO PRODUCE ENERGY
		+	AGUAS SUBTERRÁNEAS PARA REFRIGERACIÓN / GROUNDWATER FOR COOLING

Office Building

The *Office Building* at Calveen, Amersfoort (1997–2000), is located along the urban loop that serves a newly created industrial zone. It is a development composed of so-called 'generic' buildings, which are economical, simple, squarish, low quality structures which often have projecting canopies to catch the attention of passers-by.

The client requested a typical multi-storey building with a floor area of 4,000 square metres with maximum flexibility as to how the interior space could be partitioned or reorganised to respond to current or future needs. The solution proposed by MVRDV is a long seven-storey rectangular prism (54.7 x 10.5 metre footprint). On each floor the placement of a solid wall (externally faced in reddish-purple bricks) opposite a full glass wall is alternated from one side to the other. The Oregon pine windows are fastened to the round cement pillar structure as a secondary features in the image of the building façades.

A brick-faced continuous line connects the solid wall and the floors to create a back-and-forth serpentine figure on each end of the building and characterise its singular identity.

The asymmetrically-positioned utility columns contain stairways, lifts, sanitary facilities, and engineering systems. On each floor they stand away from the solid wall by 1.5 metres.

The solid walls on the two main façades support the insignia of the companies located in the building.

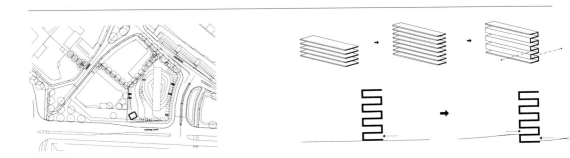

General plan

Development of the design concept

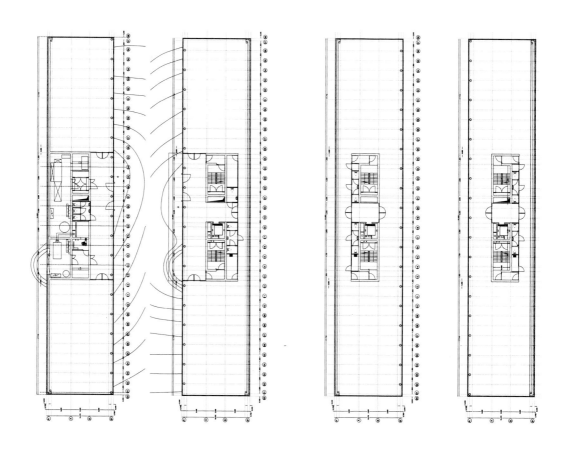

Plans at different levels
and section

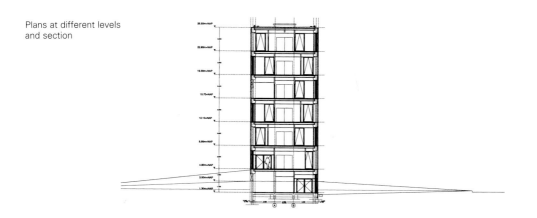

View of a wall and detail
of the opposite façade

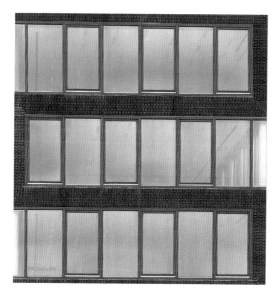

Flight Forum

Flight Forum, Eindhoven (1997–2005) is a project for an office and commercial complex in a former military area of some sixty hectares near the Eindhoven airport.

The work represents a criticism of the traditional approach to industrial parks in Holland for their low urban quality standards and especially for the excessive use of land.

The proposal thus involves grouping the buildings into clusters connected by a continuous multi-lane road dubbed 'asphalt spaghetti' for the sinuous path it follows. It is designed without intersections in order to enhance road safety.

Each structure has an entrance facing the road and a sufficiently large and accessible area for parking and goods loading/unloading. The building clusters maintain a continuity with the urban landscape and allow for larger green areas.

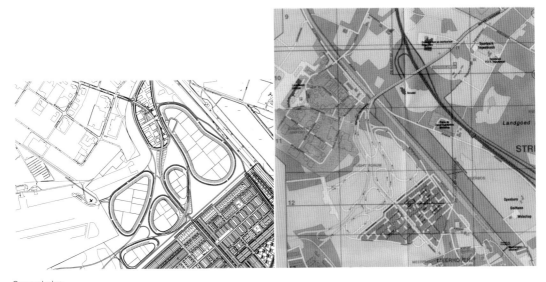

General plan

Night view

Development of the traffic
flow diagram

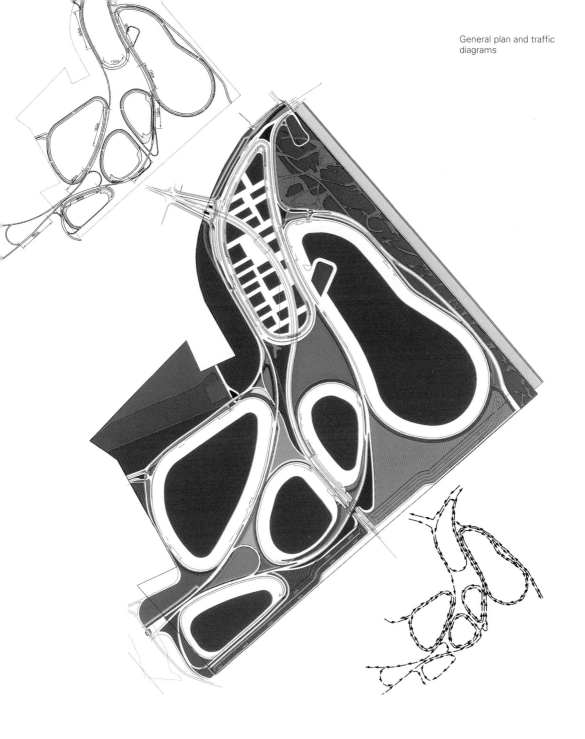

Night view of a piece
of roadway

Unterföhring Park Village

Unterföhring Park Village, Munich (1999–2004), is the masterplan for an office park situated in a commercial area northeast of Munich that is to be built in two stages. The first stage involves the construction of nine buildings, five of which are designed by MVRDV.

MVRDV's overall design comprises the construction of nineteen different buildings to achieve maximum possible density and generate an urban-type atmosphere. A 'heterogeneous' effect is achieved by having each building differ in form and finishing material.

The 'village' will occupy a vacant area in the Unterföhring Park shopping centre, which has become a new urban hub. The underground parking areas are accessed at the plaza level, which is paved in natural stone. The plaza is conceived as a gathering area and hence is off limits to vehicle traffic (with the exception of service and emergency vehicles).

The roofs of the buildings are green to create the illusion of a 'second landscape', while the buildings themselves are surrounded by trees and shrubbery.

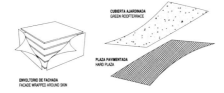

Conceptual diagram

View of one of the buildings

Sequence of elevations

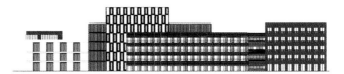

General plan

Plans of the buildings

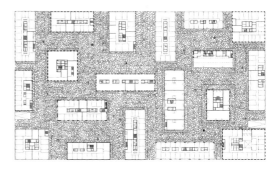

Diagram of building
densification process
and development of design
framework

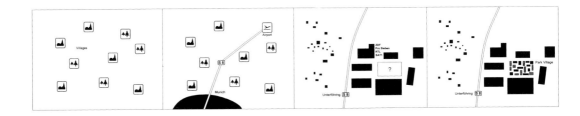

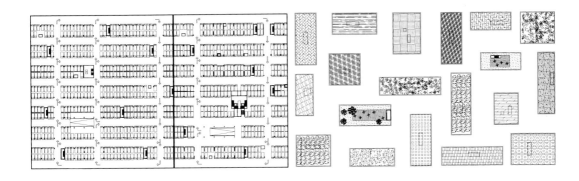

Views of model

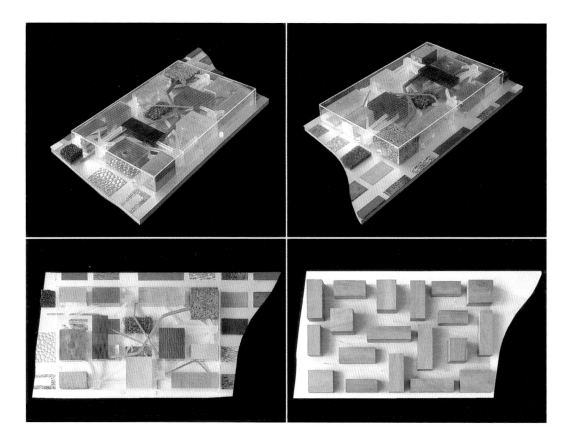

Hageneiland Housing

Hageneiland Housing, Ypenburg (2000–03) is a development with 119 dwellings which is part of the Vinex plan for Ypenburg designed by Frits Palboom and Els Bet. The plan is composed of five distinct sub-developments whose masterplans were created by different architects. Waterwijk, designed by MVRDV, is one of them. It is a district with 850 dwellings broken up into different sections (each with its own name). Hageneiland, Patio Houses, and Quattro Villa are three proposals by MVRDV for this collection of islands (only the first one has been built).

The trapezoidal area is laid out with parallel pedestrian routes that cut it into four long strips of land which are crossed by short streets composing a orderly and continuous traffic network among buildable lots of different sizes. The buildings are arranged so that they do not line up. This stratagem creates a diversified range of vistas and a perception of increased space.

The complex is oriented to young couples with children. Each dwelling has a garden and there are two playgrounds for children in the central area of the development. Cars are parked in areas around the perimeter and the inner areas are completely pedestrian.

The design concept involves a free association of a basic 'archetypical' element: a simple structure with a peaked roof, as idealised in children's imagery.[1] The standard dwellings are 121 or 130 square metres distributed on three levels. Plans call for row houses with two to eight units, some having gardens in front, some behind, and still others having a garden on both sides.

The units are also distinguished by the finishing materials (wood, corrugated sheet, stone, polyurethane panels, or tiles) with which they are completely faced, and by their colours (ivy, ochre, blue, grey, black). In keeping with Dutch tradition, the garden includes a small tool-shed/greenhouse which mimics the form of the house and can also be made with different materials: wood, bricks, or glass (if used as a greenhouse).

The broad range of spatial options offered by the project on such a limiting starting grid serves as an emblem for the achievement of 'freedom' of habitation in a flat and indeterminate land lacking any strong landmarks. MVRDV's thinking on the themes of *order* and *liberty*, *constraints* and *creativity* as exemplified in this proposal was positively received by Dutch culture. In December 2002 the work won the NAi (Netherlands Architecture Institute) architecture prize, which is awarded every two years.

[1] The three lodges for the Hoge Veluwe National Park are also based on the same archetype but involve *deformation*, while in Hageneiland it is a case of *iteration*.

View of private areas

General plan and overall
view of work

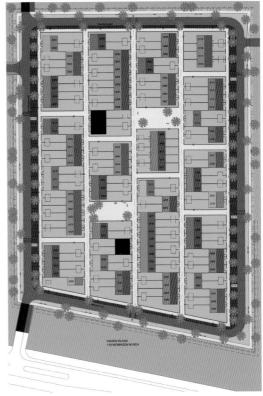

'Catalogue' of buildings

Elevations and section

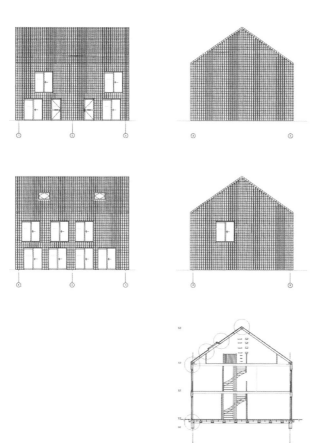

Plan and section of roof

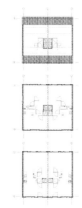

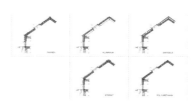

pages 98-99
View of the neighbourhood

Patio Houses

Patio Houses, Ypenburg (1999–2001) seeks to provide a design response to an 'extreme' situation created by the urban development of a highly densified society. In this context the architects see the 'garden' as the last hope for survival.

In an area adjacent to their Hageneiland project, MVRDV proposes an island development comprising a housing complex completely surrounded by a 4.5 metre wall. As in earlier works (starting with Berlin Voids whose section strangely resembles the plan of this project), each dwelling has its own form and their assembly in the delimited areas of the island-container is like the recomposition of puzzle pieces.

The houses do not have windows; light comes through the skylight-roof. Inhabitants can only see the sky; the uniform surrounding landscape is completely ignored. Access to the private patio is gained via the skylight, thus uniting discretion with the 'view of the neighbour's barbeque'.

For economic reasons the project was modified (in its place 'normal houses' were built, as MVRDV relates). Named Patio Island 2 (2001–05), it consists of a cluster of two-storey houses with slopping roofs and patios. The houses abut one another, in four staggered rows to break the excessive uniformity of the layout.

Patio Island 2. Top view.
Illustration from *KM3*

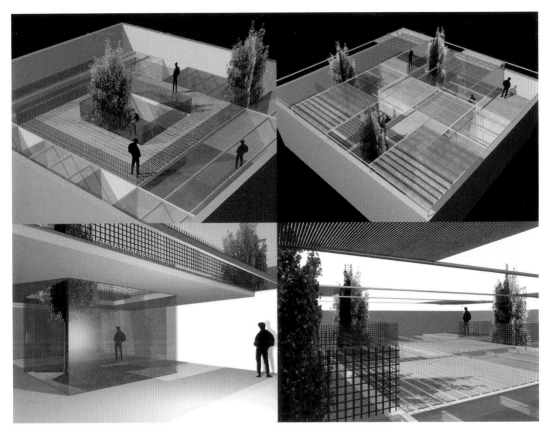

Internal spatial solutions

Patio house

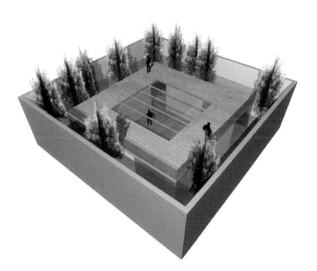

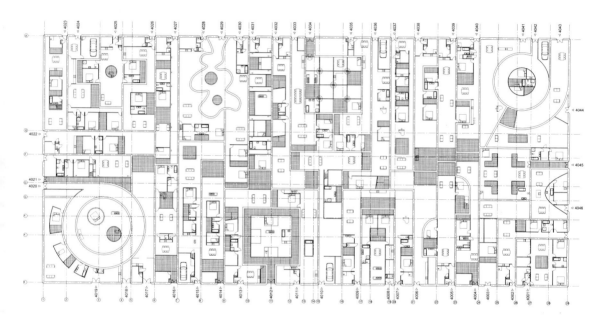

View of a patio
and floorplan solutions

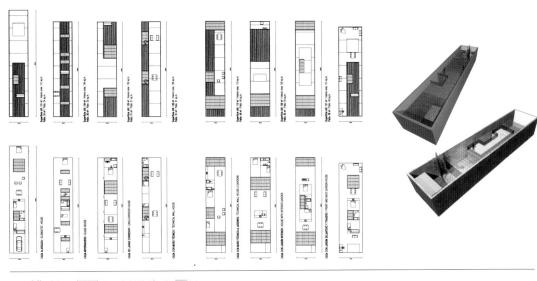

General floorplan, details
of a dwelling and floorplan
solutions

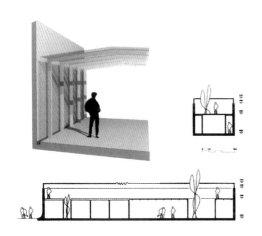

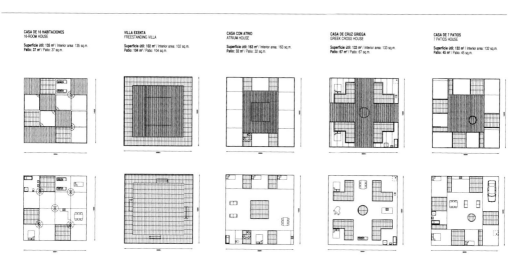

CASA DE 16 HABITACIONES
16-ROOM HOUSE

Superficie útil: 135 m² / Interior area: 135 sq.m.
Patio: 37 m² / Patio: 37 sq.m.

VILLA EXENTA
FREESTANDING VILLA

Superficie útil: 102 m² / Interior area: 102 sq.m.
Patio: 104 m² / Patio: 104 sq.m.

CASA CON ATRIO
ATRIUM HOUSE

Superficie útil: 163 m² / Interior area: 163 sq.m.
Patio: 32 m² / Patio: 32 sq.m.

CASA DE CRUZ GRIEGA
GREEK CROSS HOUSE

Superficie útil: 133 m² / Interior area: 133 sq.m.
Patio: 67 m² / Patio: 67 sq.m.

CASA DE 7 PATIOS
7 PATIOS HOUSE

Superficie útil: 132 m² / Interior area: 132 sq.m.
Patio: 45 m² / Patio: 45 sq.m.

Quattro Villa

Quattro Villa, Ypenburg (1999–2000) is a project for sixteen residences, four to a unit, for the area adjacent to Hageneiland, where the Rietvelden subdivision (2000–02) of Claus en Kaan is located.

MVRDV's idea was to create four high standing volumes in an area completely lacking in contours. They would be built at a height of twelve metres above water level, each one supported on two 'pilings', heavy reinforced concrete structures housing the lifts. The houses have only one floor, and each has a private solarium on the roof accessible via a stairway. The structures represent signals that complete and characterise the surrounding landscape.

In this case too, the project differed from the original idea due to economic reasons. The houses are not suspended, but set at water level. In addition, the Long Houses (2005) are on two levels and are entirely clad in wood. They are covered with a pitched roof and surrounded by a platform for use as a walkway.

Long Houses, view from the canal. Illustration from *KM3*

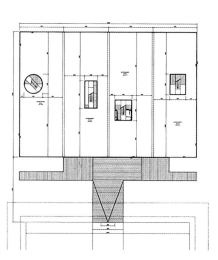

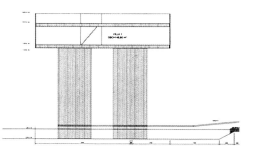

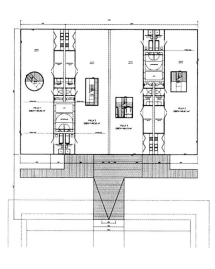

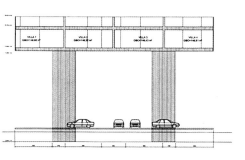

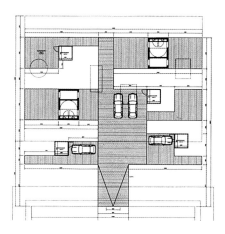

View of model

Floorplans for: Hageneiland
Housing, Patio Houses,
Quattro Villa

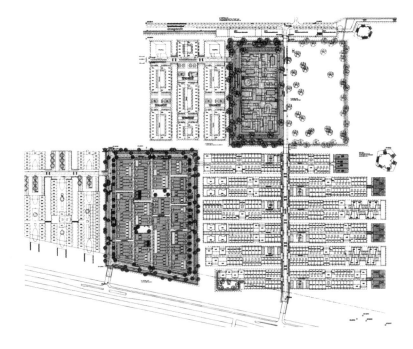

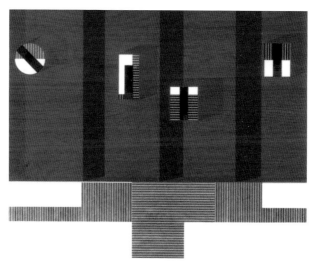

Silodam

Silodam, Amsterdam (1995–2002) is a building that looks like a sort of ship moored at the end of a dock extending into the waters of the Ij inlet. Seen from the outside, the building looks like a stack of variously coloured containers, but it is actually more complex and less linear. It contains 157 dwellings in a mixed format (efficiencies, lofts, apartments with patios, maisonettes) along with offices, workshops, commercial structures, public facilities, and common areas.

The need to develop a significant variety of spatial arrangements led the architects to regulate the many solutions via the institution of mini dwelling units composed of four to eight similar apartments constructed of the same material, and having the same colour and façade fixture design. Internally the same spatial and chromatic differentiation characterise vestibules and corridors. Other variations of the units regard their width (from 5 to 15 metres), depth (partial, total, or dual level), floor height (from 2.80 to 3.80 metres), number of rooms (from one to five), additional spaces (greenhouses, courtyards, patios, common areas), access ways (bridges, stairways, galleries, corridors), and also structural characteristics (partition walls, round reinforced concrete or steel pillars).

The multiplicity of closely interrelated functions inside the building and the range of its options and flows, united with its suggestive placement—isolated and central with respect to the city's historical nucleus—represent an important redefinition of the MVRDV concept of 'freedom'. This group of apartments and services, in spite of their objective concentration in a container, gives the impression of wanting to offer the same balance and spatial autonomy as the traditional house with a garden. It is an idea that grows out of a careful study of the *Unité d'habitation*, as well as out of the curiosity and punctilio to go beyond the rigidity of Le Corbusier's spatial layout, seeking to 'break' the constraints (in a purely conceptual sense) of that closed volume.

View of east façade and elevations

General plan

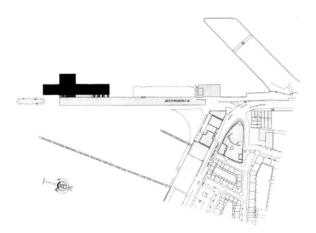

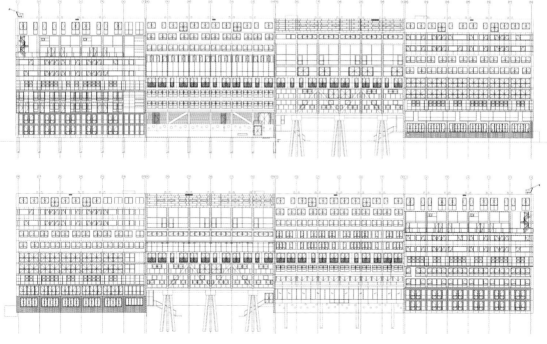

View of east façade

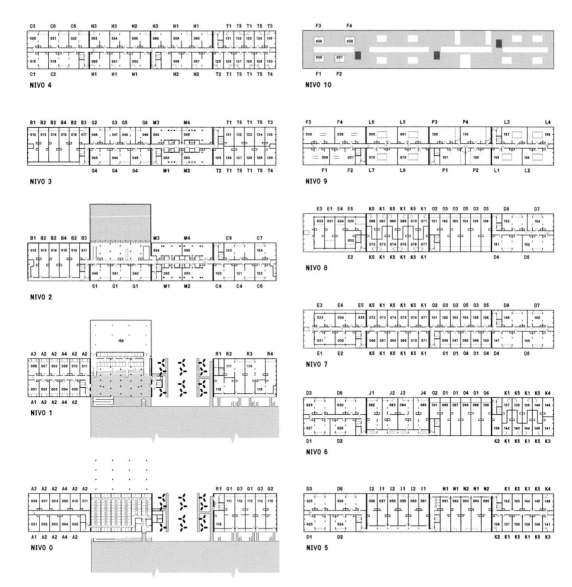

NIVO 4

NIVO 3

NIVO 2

NIVO 1

NIVO 0

NIVO 10

NIVO 9

NIVO 8

NIVO 7

NIVO 6

NIVO 5

View of the dock

Portion of the façade

View of the south façade

View of the observation
deck

Detail of metal pillars

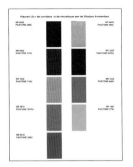

Catalogue of colours of the various sectors

Internal route

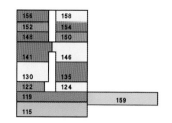

Layout of spatial units

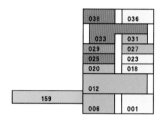

Corridor solutions

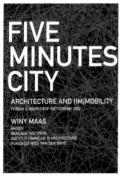

Left
Illustration from
Metacity/Datatown

After *Farmax* and *Metacity/Datatown*, the first two important studies, MVRDV in 1998 began to publish other works at a sustained pace, each directed to a specific research topic. 'There was a natural development in the overall research. It was as though one topic always suggested or at least uncovered the next. The public aspect in the development of this work stimulated and encouraged critical reflection. As such over the years this element became an integral part in the process of development in the various topics, from *Farmax* to *Metacity/Datatown*, from *3D City*, *Pig City*, *Functionmixer*, to *Agromixer* and *Regionmaker*. The same happened with the project on satellites, which is probably the most interesting work produced by the Berlage Institute'.[1]

A substantial part of these books brings together work produced for exhibitions, video installations, seminars and workshops, or they constitute research and development carried out internally, and with the contribution of European universities. In addition, they are the fruit of work commissioned by municipalities, provinces or governments (Switzerland, North Brabant, Rotterdam, Catalonia, Holland etcetera), and developed in association with economists, geographers and planners and directed to urban realities which in their macroscopic development—having reached a critical point from the environmental and social point of view—require the formulation, visualisation and verification of viable possibilities for intervention.

This is a new way for the architect to tackle a project's course, beginning with a different way of interpreting the notion of *context* and organising fact-finding inquiries and the proposal for intervention. 'Architects, more than in the past, have the opportunity of using a vast range of communicative possibilities through various kinds and levels of expression.

They can work not only on buildings, but also on regional planning; they can work in the fields of research and education, in the theatre, on art installations and political programs. As a result, possibilities at a regional and global level can be visualised, as in *Costa Iberica* or *Stadtland Schweiz*. In addition, alternatives to current trends can be promoted, as in Pig City'.[2]

As noted, the series of theoretical works produced by MVRDV is extremely vast; however, before considering projects over the last four years, it is useful to look at some of the most important studies: *Costa Iberica*, *Brabant City 2050*, *Pig City*, *KM3/The 3D City* (1997–2001), *The Functionmixer*, *The Regionmaker*, *Five Minutes City*, and the most recent, *KM3*.

Costa Iberica (1998) considers the theme of density in relation to a real context.[3] It deals with the high-density band of housing surrounding the Iberian Peninsula that developed without interruption along the coast in total ignorance of responsibilities of an ecological-environmental nature. It constitutes a macroscopic 'linear city' with the singular characteristic of being entirely dedicated to leisure; in fact the book's subheading is *Upbeat to the Leisure City*.

The reality considered by MVRDV is, therefore, that of a 'continuous city' springing from affluence and globalisation's productive gains. Within the last fifty years the coast has become the densest area in Europe (equal to New York or Hong Kong), due to the irresistible attraction (for cold countries) of sun, sea, food, freedom and low prices. However, such uncontrolled development lacks residential blocks, offices, industry, business districts, museums, theatres and universities; there are only cafeterias, restaurants and hotels; '[...] it is as real as it is virtual, a city that exists and does not exist. It is a sublime "Fata morgana", a kind of European Las Vegas surrounding the Iberian Meseta.'[4]

Despite initial success, development along the coast has now come to a halt and is slowly heading for crisis resulting from competition from other exotic (or cheaper) countries.

In the presence of the enormous potential for development of this reality, which in perspective the authors see as very close to the Californian one, the course for a worthwhile project for change needs to be identified. And so '[...] it could be transformed into a more sustainable and sophisticated example of the leisure city.'[5] It could be a prototype for the post-industrial city that frees itself from the rule of place and enters into the realm of pure hedonism.

In substance, according to MVRDV, it is necessary to reconsider what exists and adopt diverse programs that modify the mono-functional component that no longer relies solely on tourism but is directed to leisure time, in which work and domestic life are based (on the Sydney and San Francisco models). This would be accompanied by a series of interventions

Illustration from
Costa Iberica

beginning with the possibility of urban regeneration (directed especially to areas built during the 1970s and 1980s). The aim is to partly renew these structures, creating spaces for agriculture, industry, offices, cultural institutions and housing.

The research and proposals contained in *Costa Iberica* aim to critically cast a glance at the unhealthy conditions of modern society and propose a method of analysis to apply to development. The study conclusively shows how today architecture plays a limited role, because it is society (seen as a whole with its complexities and contradictions) that shapes the environment.

Brabant City 2050 (1998) examines possible ways to reorganise Brabant, a region in Holland bordering Belgium, especially in relation to residential-settlement aspects and production activities. Thanks to its attractive landscape, characterised by woods and vast rural areas, it has undergone intense residential-industrial development, following a trend that makes living and working in such places attractive. As a consequence, numerous though small villages with residential and industrial areas, highways, commercial centres and cultural and service facilities etcetera have been built. These small, very similar urban centres scattered throughout the entire regional territory have produced a 'carpet of sameness'.

In this study, MVRDV's aim was to identify a way through this situation of stalemate (and 'mediocrity') by seeking to expand the area's future economic development without losing (but, rather, boosting) its agricultural-naturalistic character.

The central point of the proposal is based on the idea of unitary recomposition of the fragmented ensemble of municipalities through a single new municipality with the responsibility of guiding the process of transformation and 'conglomeration' of diverse realities. This involves the demolition of residential or industrial settlements (in order to allow as much

131

expansion as possible in vacant territory) and reconstruction in more appropriate areas (to achieve greater urban continuity), preserving, at the same time, the specific characteristics of each centre. The result is a patchwork of distinct identities that constitute the 'suburbs' of Brabant City.

Pig City (2000–01) is a study looking at a fundamental issue of an ecological nature. Starting with data collected at the Agricultural University of Wageningen, architects produced an interesting investigative study to verify the possibility of development of one of Holland's most important agricultural production activities: that of pig farming. Statistics maintain that in 1999 the number of inhabitants in the country equalled the number of pigs. Each animal requires a 664 sq m area, including space for production and feed storage (natural and industrial). The trend to prefer biological feed would increase the relevant area to 1,726 sq m. The consequence of this is that in the future 75% of Dutch territory could be taken up entirely by pig farming.

The double aim of MVRDV's proposal is to dramatically highlight the imminent danger of an environmental and social hazard and to offer a possible solution by recovering (in an apparently surreal form) the necessary space for this activity. The verticalisation of production structures proposed, through the creation of large abattoirs-silos able to contain all phases of the cycle relating to raising, production, fertiliser recycling and food stockpiling, aims to support growth in animal production and encourage the least possible waste of surface area, avoiding the risk of epidemics.

KM3/The 3D City (2001) is a study developed in a university environment; its aim is to find a solution to excessive building production (warehouses, structures for stockpiling goods, offices) which in part have 'disfigured' the traditional image of the country causing increases in land costs and stimulating increasingly greater investment. The project has a three-dimensional configuration (instead of the traditional two-dimensional one) and aims to recover new (and unusual) possibilities for extra space. It is an attempt to '[...] create a utopian city with the aim of anticipating problems relating to world population increases and environmental protection.'[6]

The cities examined are Amsterdam and Rotterdam. The stimulus to give shape to spectacular cities led the authors to mix '[...] images of Archizoom's *No-Stop City*, Superstudio's *Monumento continuo*, ARCHIGRAM's *Walking City* and Ludwig Hilberseimer's *Großstadtarchitektur*; or scenes from films such as Fritz Lang's *Metropolis* and Jean-Jacques Beineix's *The Fifth Element*'.[7]

Rotterdam, as a result of Second World War bombing, lost the markers of its historic building fabric, and as a result, also lost the obstacles to regulating in a careful and sensitive way the developmental process of urban densification. The study tackles the issue of developing areas next to large road axis, creating road systems running parallel to current ones. The new urban landscape is a system of suspended, aerial and ventilated layers that are superimposed, at one moment in shadow and then in light, that is able to respond to diverse functional programs.

Amsterdam on the other hand, was able to preserve its historic centre, due to heritage conservation regulations that directed new urban development to the outskirts, leaving the heart of the city to cultural and tourism activities. In this case the possibility for intervention is reversed with respect to the previous one in that the MVRDV proposal is to excavate beneath the centre (based on a vision that had been put forward by Winy Maas and Jacob van Rijs in *Icebergs*, a text from 1995[8]), realising a system of urban connections like a continuous fly-over system, an articulation of voids and views, a system in which the old city is above the new, and which by virtue of being underground is dark and shadowy: a Gotham City of the new millennium.

The Functionmixer (2001) is based on the theme of the outdated mode of planning by functionally specialised areas; this is replaced by the introduction of sophisticated technology in the production process, creating new opportunities, allowing work areas to mix with residential, and in so doing overcoming the negative effects of mono-cultural developments. This trend is pursued not only by the Dutch government but also by the real estate market itself, which favours function-mix and the creation of multiple spaces.

All this necessitates a paradigm change able to deal with space shortage and diversify widespread uniformity. This requires identifying new models for a different way of dealing with environmental reality, in which various functions and densities can co-exist.

Software was developed to achieve this aim, with the intention of determining suitable function-mix models. The peculiar nature of this program, compared with others currently available directed to circumscribed thematic spheres, is that it is a dynamic product, pre-programmed to put together radically different situations. MVRDV writes that, '*Functionmixer* is a heuristic model enabling us to identify the best project in a sea of possible candidates. The best is the circumscribed result according to chosen parameters'.[9] This allows for interacting in a 'discussion room', providing possibilities for creating diverse urban scenarios. 'It is based on the decomposition of the environment into function units which in their qualitative definition as configurative elements (walls, floors, ceilings) find their right neighbour. The software rapidly develops millions of possible combinations: it lines them up, and gives the best solution with respect to given needs; it can be used to compare solutions; it shows existing laws and their limitations; and it facilitates discussion of possible obligatory changes in plans, coverage and regulations.'[10]

The Regionmaker (2002) is a study of problems relating to development in the Rhine-Ruhr, a region in southern Germany. The book is part of an exhibition with the same title that took place in the NRW-Forum Kultur und Wirtschaft in Düsseldorf (between mid November 2002 and mid February 2003). The study has two aims: on the one hand to present and identify the regional entity as a new urban dimension and as a competing tool in a world that appears boundless, and on the other to formulate possibilities for development in this specific German region.

The study is a significant change in project size (the urban scale is superseding the architectonic one), and its tools must change to accommodate the effects of globalisation. The close collaborative ties that are being formed between European countries and the introduction of Euro have led to enormous changes on the Continent. Nations appear to be dissolving. A new 'order' is emerging, made up of agglomeration and dispersion. As complexities become more intense, it is necessary to identify which method or stratagem can best be adopted. It is difficult to formulate possibilities; perhaps it is more useful to develop an objective method that can be used from different points of view in order to develop knowledge going beyond the exigencies of the moment.

The production of visualisation and spatialisation tools for hypothetical projects on a regional scale is becoming increasingly necessary in order to create a 'new context' to reconfigure. It is necessary to build comprehensible structures in order to understand and conceptualise the present and so communicate it.

MVRDV has recently received commissions from different European governments, provinces and municipalities (Switzerland, North Brabant, Oslo, Rotterdam, Catalonia and Holland) to work with economists, geographers and planners on regional identity and on potential future programs (all supported by appropriate visualisation).

The Rhine-Ruhr region has dramatically lost its identity. It is primarily known for its heavy industry, which developed during the Second World

War. Situated in an area on the edge of Middle Europe, it lacks meaningful identity and a strong centrality. It does not have a high density though it is highly populated. Each area is equally accessible as it has an extensive network of highways.

Rhine--Ruhr can therefore be seen as the first stage of this process. Its development occurred through collaboration between MVRDV and various academic and professional institutions. The result of this collaboration, as summarised by Maas in the book's introductory chapter, is the creation of software called *Regionmaker*—based on the experience of *Functionmixer*—which functions as a 'dynamic presentation device' showing future scenarios of territorial reality beginning with the Rhine--Ruhr region.

On the contrary, the book can be considered a manual for *Regionmaker* and its applications in the Rhine--Ruhr area, an 'optimistic' tool in which it represents a dream rather than a reality complete in itself. In substance it is the 'prototype of a far-ranging tool that oscillates as it steers a course between globalism and regionalism'.

KM3 (2005) is MVRDV's most recent theoretical effort. The book's theme is announced in the cover's subtitle: 'Three-dimensionality can be considered a fundamental aspect of architecture, the profession's acclaimed dominion. In times of globalisation and expansion of scale, it is time to update definition: metres are being transformed into kilometres, M3 becomes KM3'. In conclusion, at the end of the long road, the authors add a kind of concise definition to the work: 'Exploratory travels in capacity'.

It is, in the end, a substantial volume that develops the theme of *density*, and is a direct continuation of the previous work, *Farmax*. In this instance however, the same basic theme is analysed from a different viewpoint, that of 'three-dimensionality', allowing a move away from the narrow condition of 'urban pessimism' towards an exploration of 'some new places of application'.

In this way, a still limited kind of statistic analysis of the Dutch territory (that referred to in *Farmax*) now has the power of adopting a 'pure intensity' value, as Maas declares, expanding in a global dimension. *KM3*, therefore, is the real and symbolic representation of a dimensional/spatial change: from cubic-metre to cubic-kilometre (as the authors contend).

The book, conceived as a file organised in ten chapters, can be divided concisely into two parts. The first (corresponding to the first seven chapters) contains research undertaken by MVRDV in collaboration with the Berlage Institute on the theme of regional planning and the 3D City in the period between 1997 and 2003. In this part the theme of *density* is considered on a global scale, highlighting the contradictions in the vortical increase in development (and its attendant infrastructure) that lacks adequate control and self-regulating instruments. 'What is the solution to the oppressive process of global space consumption?' asks Maas, 'What power can 'absorb' this minimal level, this two-dimensional 'state', slowing it and inducing it to follow a more cohesive environmental condition? Can new cities avoid creating enormous peripheries, pending new colonisation? Can we impose the issue of density, which in the end could lead to more productive cities? [...] More synergy, efficiency and mix would bring greater social contact, civility and opportunities for architecture. In the end, what kind of urban planning will appear? In an age that continues to be dominated by zoning—a very two-dimensional approach—can urban planning in the third dimension develop in its own way? Can a city be built by actually creating more public levels, expanding the capacities of the existing urban area?'.[11]

In the second part this general view returns to the specific themes examined by the studio over the past ten years. The sequence of works selected according to spatial viewpoint (on the basis of themes: communication, inclination, cumulation, curvature, expulsion, internalisation, launching, reduction etcetera) is a record of the studio's activities, but it is above all a select case study of works achieved and of proposals re-read and filtered through a new project dimension realised by adopting the notion of 'three-dimensionality' within the ideational process.

'This book defines a repertoire of buildings that can be of some use', observes Maas, 'and proposes software as one of possible tools for navigating through this enlarged complexity. It can be read as an attempt to go deeper in relation to some of our earlier positions'.[12]

[1] Cristina Díaz Moreno, Efrén García Grinda, op. cit.

[2] Winy Maas, 'Architecture is a Device', in Véronique Patteeuw (edited by), op. cit., 143–44.

[3] This book, like the earlier ones, was conceived by Maas and produced by MVRDV; the work is based on a series of studies carried out in spring 1998 with students of Esarq in Barcelona during a three-week workshop.

[4] Winy Maas, Costa Iberica, in MVRDV, Costa Iberica. Upbeat to the Leisure City, Actar, Barcelona 1998, p. 73.

[5] Ibidem, p. 173.

[6] Bart Lootsma, op. cit., p. 47.

[7] Ibidem.

[8] Winy Maas, Jacob van Rijs, Icebergs, in MVRDV, Farmax... op. cit.

[9] MVRDV, 'The Functionmixer' art. cit.

[10] MVRDV, Five Minutes City. Architecture and [Im]mobility, Episode Publishers, Rotterdam 2003, p. 134.

[11] MVRDV, KM3, Actar, Madrid 2005, pp. 270–71.

[12] Winy Maas, 'Km3. La densità al potere', interview by Manuela Martorelli with Winy Maas, in Il Giornale dell'Architettura, no. 36, January 2006.

MVRDV

Three-dimensionality can be seen as architecture's fundamental existence, the profession's acclaimed domain. In times of globalization and scale enlargement, an update of this definition seems needed: meters turn into kilometers, M3 becomes

KM3

Excursions on Capacities

Some of the operations on which MVRDV projects are based:
1. communicate
2. connect
3. extrude
4. rotate
5. hang
6. lift

Recent Works

In this last group of projects, some of which have remained pure theory, others built or under construction, we see MVRDV's desire to focus attention on thematic pairs that seem to be the 'sublimation' of some of those examined previously, such as congestion and individual freedoms, mobility and environmental safeguards, and the contradistinction between building interiors and exteriors.

Mirador, Sanchinarro,
2001–04. View of terrace

Central Library

Central Library in Brabant (2000) is a project presented at the 8th Venice Biennial Architecture Exhibition *Next* (2002). The project appears to be the ideal continuation of *Brabant City 2050*. It is an operation that 'condenses' the numerous small libraries spread around the territory (as a reflection of 1960s cultural policy) into a single structure. Over the years this approach has lost efficacy both for budget constraints, which limited the possibilities for purchasing new books, and due to the spread of urbanisation, which modified relations with users by creating needs that were not met by the services offered. The enormous growth in new information supports such as CDs and computers has placed information on anything at people's fingertips, wherever they are. Hence, in spite of the possible shift away from paper as a support as a result of the crisis in the current way the service is organised, MVRDV proposed a new strategy for setting it up.

The architects' proposal is to combine all the collections of the small libraries into a single structure where people can meet and mingle and exchange information. The library, equipped with a book storage facility on a par with European standards, will also have to have an appropriate distribution system and maximum direct access by users. Hence the building is conceived as a continuous wall of books coiled around itself and circumscribing a central area. From there a seventeen-kilometre walk leads to the summit of the huge tower-cylinder. The enormous central space is a place for people to spend time (with a cafeteria and other services) offering a view of the entire collection and of the surrounding landscape.

Hypothetical
urban/territorial setting

Floorplans at different
levels

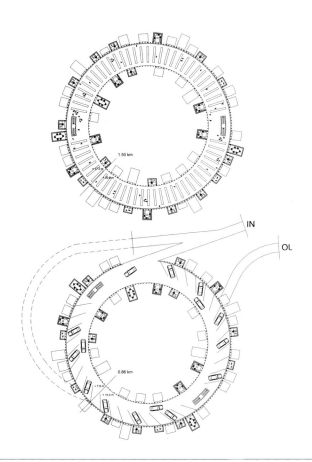

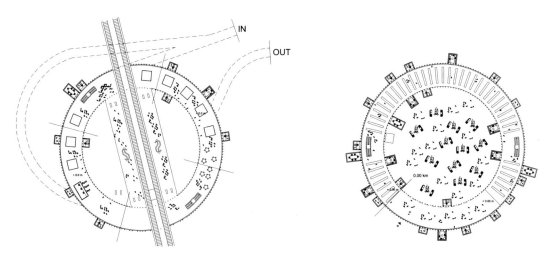

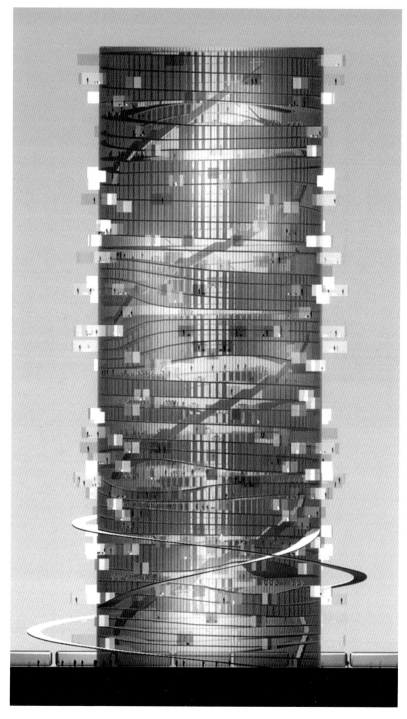

Silicon Hill

Silicon Hill in Stockholm (2000) is a proposal for meeting two different design needs: finding an image to represent the new central office of the Swedish Post (previously state-run but now liberalised) and the new way of organising the service; and safeguarding the hill where the work will be built, the last remaining undeveloped natural area in central Stockholm.

Regarding the significance of that operation, especially in relation to the ecological theme that determined the characteristic imprint of the project, the authors say they look at nature simply as an urban activity. It is one of the necessities for survival, for oxygen uptake, for producing food and animals, for recreation, and for psychological reasons.[1]

The conservation of the natural topography with its complement of trees is the starting point on the conceptual pathway of this project. MVRDV imagines they can lift the surface layer of the earth as if it were a cloth by grasping it at two different points (corresponding to the two hilltops). By literally lifting the land, the existing nature becomes part of the programme.[2] This operation of detaching the 'skin' from the underlying rocky substrate creates an empty space which is augmented by excavating into the granite below. The conceptual 'in between' that is created provides enough volume to meet the needs expressed by the client, which are: an underground parking structure, offices, common areas, utilities, a restaurant, a sauna, and an auditorium. The interior space is resolved with terraces on different levels that gives the whole a graduated set of spatial situations, from common areas to private zones. Inside one of the two peaks there is a restaurant with a terrace roof offering open-air dining. The auditorium is located under the other one. Outside, in the central basin, there is a pool of water and a sauna.

[1] Cristina Díaz Moreno, Efrén García Grinda, op. cit.
[2] MVRDV, 'Silicon Hill', *El Croquis*, no. 111, 2002.

View of proposed design

145

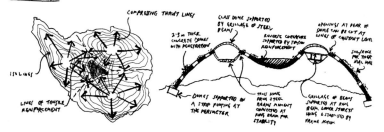

CONCRETE DOMES

ISO LINES

LINES OF TENSILE
REINFORCEMENT

COMPRESSING THRUST LINES

2-3 m THICK
CONCRETE DOMES
WITH PENETRATION

DOMES SUPPORTED ON
A STRIP FOOTING AT
THE PERIMETER

GLASS DOME SUPPORTED
BY GRILLAGE OF STEEL
BEAMS

REVERSE CURVATURE
SUPPORTED BY TENSION
REINFORCEMENT

TRUSS HUNG
FROM STEEL
BEAM: MOMENT
CONNECTED AT
RING BEAM FOR
STABILITY

OPENINGS AT PEAK OF
DOME CAN BE CUT AT
LINES OF CONSTANT LOAD

SILL/ROCK
FOR THE
WALL WALL

GRILLAGE OF BEAMS
SUPPORTED AT RING
BEAM, LOWER STOREYS
HUNG & STABILISED BY
FRAME ACTION

Cúpulas de hormigón. Diagramas estructurales
Concrete domes. Structural diagrams

Exterior and interiors
of proposed design

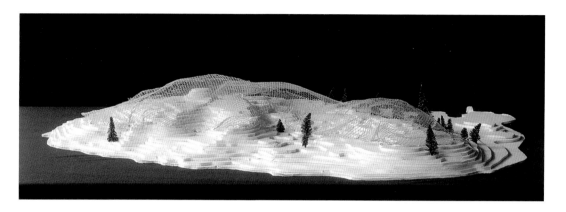

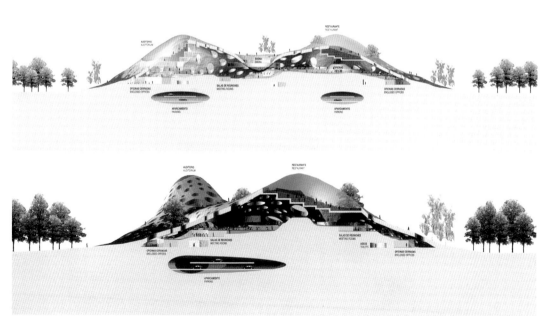

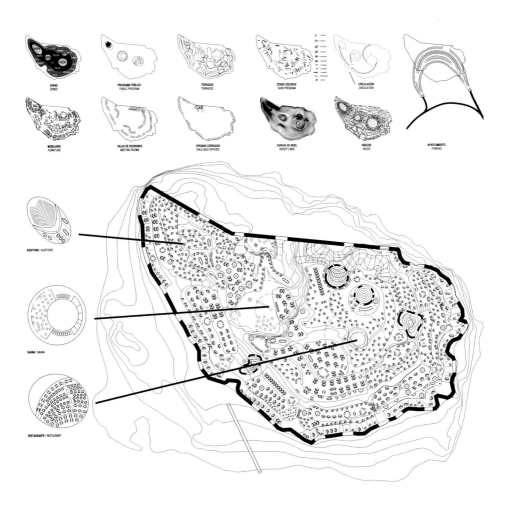

Media Galaxy

Media Galaxy in New York (2001–02) regards the MVRDV proposal, elaborated with Garison Siegel, for the new Eyebeam Institute, which deals with the 'ephemeral and fluid' world of mass media. The works of art created using this means require an exhibition structure that transcends the traditional schemes, a completely new type of space where they can be collected and presented to the public.

The museum designed by MVRDV subtly interprets the specificity of this condition, creating a fluid and continuous space. It is a complex structure that is a centre for artistic research, production, and consumption. The structure is a hollow tower composed of a double perforated skin that serves as a support for a system of continuous projections. The empty space also contains rooms of different sizes which can be used for a host of different purposes. They vary in height and width and can be closed off or provided with panoramic views of the world outside.

The architects consider this type of building to be a sort of 'refuge'. Its floorplan is fairly recurrent in their design, and they have known how to create spatial solutions that are always highly varied, imaginative, and captivating. The volume is conceived from the inside out in a conceptual process that the architects equate with the way certain automobiles were designed, such as the Renault Espace, Scenic, and Twingo. The designers sought to maximise internal possibilities by working initially with internal dimensions and conditions. The result is a car whose exterior is determined by its internal qualities and not by the pluses and minuses of the commercial allure of its body design.[1]

[1] Cristina Díaz Moreno, Efrén García Grinda, op. cit.

Interior views

Urban setting of building

STOR
SELF
1-800-
EN

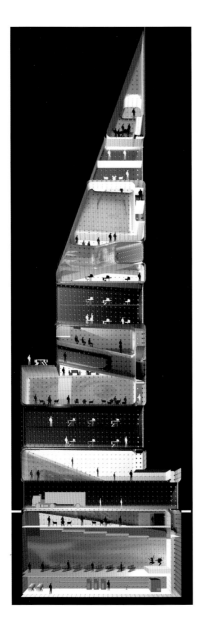

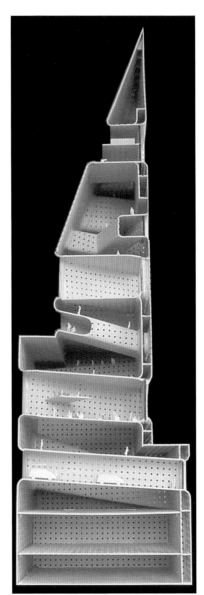

Donau City (Kissing Towers)

Donau City (Kissing Towers) in Vienna (2002) is a project for the 'city of the Danube' comprising a group of towers standing on a plinth which contains the infrastructure.

The project was inspired by critical thinking about skyscrapers, an icon of urban life and its density. Its main drawback is its isolation caused by the lack of a direct relationship with urban traffic network. The network of routes that are laid out inside of it is like a 'fabric' of dead end streets.

The resolution of the negative conditions inherent to this building type in MVRDV's view lies in the possibility of disrupting that introversion by bringing the level of the city up to the upper floors of the structure.

Hence, availing themselves of the potentials offered by new technology, the architects propose a complex of towers folded at different angles in order to obtain a range of reciprocal 'contacts' and 'conjunctions'. They also create levels that intersect them at various heights where they incorporate new functions such as vestibules, recreation areas, stores, museums, and conference rooms.

The result is a three dimensional city, solitude reshaped into expanded opportunities for socialising on the part of the inhabitants, a vertical neighbourhood with streets, squares, vestibules, and aerial level-crossings.

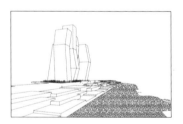 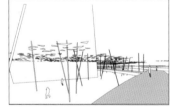 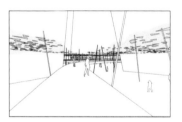

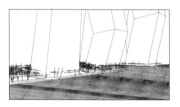 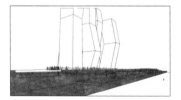 

Studies of contexts
for the towers

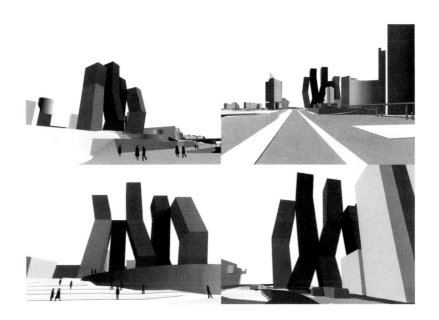

Catalogue of project
hypotheses

View of models

Final plan

View of models

General plan

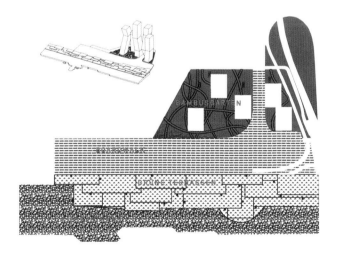

Mirador

Mirador, in Sanchinarro (2001–04), is the name of a residential building whose imposing form dominates the vast and desolate territory of the northeast outskirts of Madrid. The twenty-two-storey tower is atypical for its width and for the large hole in it starting at the twelfth floor, a sort of enormous mirador. From this 'raised plaza' you can see the Guadarrama Mountains on one side and the recent and disorderly urban sprawl of Madrid sliced by heavily trafficked thoroughfares on the other. Because of its large area, this privileged observation platform serves as a meeting place for residents of the superblock.

The project originally included a direct connection with the surrounding neighbourhood by means of an escalator that was not built. It would have descended from the belvedere level down to the public square below, an open space left free by the upward development of the building.

The objective of the building was twofold: the first regarded breaking up the orderless uniformity of the new outskirts by means of a powerful presence that was capable of giving formal and conceptual value to the surrounding cityscape and standing as an iconic landmark for the entire city; the second was the desire to further innovative research into large buildings.

With this project, realised by MVRDV together with the collaboration of Blanca Lleó Asociados, the architects provide an intelligent and meaningful response to the theme of living in an intensive residential structure without subjecting the resident to the uniform, serial logic of a rationalist-style structure. They thus recover broad margins of freedom in the variety of lodging types, designed on the basis of the individual needs of tenants (childless couples, young people sharing an apartment, transient or temporary residents, family structures in flux, senior citizens, people who work out of their homes, people who are out of the house all day, etc.). The building also offers its residents high standards in terms of habitable space, natural light, panoramic views, and the comfort of the fixtures.

The architects thus propose nine residential blocks conceived as mini neighbourhoods assembled around the 'void' space of the panoramic observation deck. They are connected by a system of vertical routes, painted orange, that transform within each residential block in order to adapt to its characteristics. The heterogeneity of the structure is highlighted by a varying pattern on the elevations as well as by the use of different materials, textures, and colours on the façades.

Inclusion of building
in the neighbourhood

View of model with
escalator

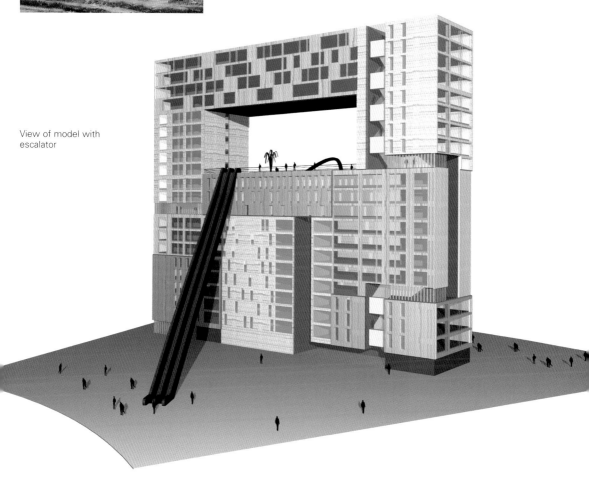

View of building

Biographies

The MVRDV studio was founded in Rotterdam in 1991. Its founders are Winy Maas, Jakob van Rijs, and Nathalie de Vries.

Winy Maas was born in Schijndel in 1959 and studied landscape architecture from 1978 to 1983 at the RHSTL in Boskoop. In 1984 he moved to the Department of Architecture and Urban Planning at the Delft University of Technology, where he received a degree in architecture and urban planning with top marks in 1990.
He leads courses and workshops in universities and institutions of many countries such as the AA of London, the Berlage Institute of Amsterdam, the Cooper Union of New York, and the universities of Delft, Eindhoven, Berlin, Barcelona, Oslo, Los Angeles, Chicago, Boston, and Princeton. From 1994 to 1997 he was a member of the editorial staff of *Forum*, from 1995 to 1997 he was a member of the board of *Items*, and since 1998 he has been a member of the steering committee of the National Design Group.

Jacob van Rijs was born in Amsterdam in 1964 and studied from 1983 to 1984 at the Free Academy of The Hague and at the Department of Architecture of the Delft University of Technology, where he graduated with top marks in 1990 and with honourable mention by Archiprix.
He leads courses and workshops in a variety of universities and institutions such as the Delft University of Technology, the Architecture Academy of Amsterdam, the Architecture Academy of Rotterdam, the AA of London, Cooper Union in New York, Rice University in Texas, TN Probe in Tokyo, and the universities of Madrid and Barcelona.

Nathalie de Vries was born in Appingedam in 1965 and studied at the Delft University of Technology, where she graduated in 1990 with top marks. She has held conferences in many countries. Since August 2005 she has been Railroad Architect for ProRail/NS. From 2002 to 2004 she was guest professor at the Berlin University of Technology. Since 2005 she has been Morgenstern Visiting Critic at the Chicago IIT. She has taught at the Berlage Institute of Rotterdam, at the ABK of Arnhem, and at the Delft University of Technology.
Since 2003 she has been a member of the Gestaltungsbeirat of Salzburg; since 2004 she has sat on the committee of founders of the Dutch architecture journal *Oase*; from 1999 to June 2005 she was a member of the board of the Netherlands Architecture Fund.

Bibliography

FARMAX, 010 Publishers, Rotterdam 1999
The study was spurred by Holland's high population density (among the highest in the world) and the low residential density in the suburban areas that tends to transform the country into a sort of 'continuous city'. MVRDV's suggestion, developed with students from the Technological University of Delft, is to implant ultra dense areas in pastoral landscapes. The book sets out to explore the prospects and limitations. This is the world of the 'extreme Floor Area Ratio', i.e., FAR MAX. The hefty volume seeks to highlight thinking on the development of the counterdistinction between building and landscape, and what happens when this relationship is reorganised or reinvented. On the one hand the architectural object tends to stand as an ideal extension of the landscape, while on the other, it aims to merge into a new, more complex structure that will incorporate it.

MVRDV at VPRO, Actar, Madrid 1999
Since 1998, an unusual building designed by the team of architects MVRDV are the premises of VPRO, one of the main broadcasting companies in the Netherlands. The design process and the present VPRO building, plus an extension project inside the Hilversum Mediapark, are shown in the book. But architecture can also be reviewed in other, non-conventional ways, as this book highlights. Hence an additional theme in this book is the everyday life in the VPRO building, presented as short stories written by a selection of authors. These stories are like sitcoms that recount events in the villa, melding together media and architecture. Big Brother already existed in this book before it became a TV hit.

Metacity/Datatown, 010 Publishers, Rotterdam, 1999
The authors wonder whether we can understand the contemporary city at a time when globalisation has expanded its scale beyond our grasp. The profound transformation has caused operators to lose control of its quantities and magnified difficulties in analysing and manipulating its components.
One possible route for getting a grasp on current reality is to employ a sophisticated information gathering process that results in a city described exclusively by data. But it is a city with no topography, no prescribed ideology, no representation, no context. The book seeks to explore the possible agenda for architecture and urban planning suggested by such a numerical approach. *Metacity/Datatown* was conceived by Winy Maas. It has been researched and produced by MVRDV.

Costa Iberica, Actar, Madrid 2000
The Spanish and Portuguese coastal area has become a tremendous economic success. In fifty years it has turned into the densest 'city' in Europe due to a series of attractions that are lacking elsewhere: sun, sea, food, freedom, cheapness. But despite these huge advantages and its endless expansion, it is condemned for its monocultural behaviour, for its lack of history, taste and culture, its overwhelming hegemony over natural resources, its total disregard for ecological responsibility. This controversy freezes its potential rather than activating it. For MVRDV, this paradoxical phenomenon that teeters between disgust and allure, between attraction and repulsion, could be transformed into a more productive approach by capitalising on its massive values, enabling the area to be turned into a more sustainable and elaborate example of the Leisure City.

The Regionmaker /RheinRuhrCity, Hatje Cantz, Düsseldorf 2002
The book accompanies an exhibition of the same name held at the NRW-Forum Kultur und Wirtschaft in Düsseldorf in 2002–03. Both the exhibition and the book seek to generate a discussion on the possible future of the Rhine-Ruhr region in Germany. The Regionmaker has been developed as an innovative planning device and has been applied to the Rhine-Ruhr urban agglomeration. It represents a significant change in dimension (urban planning instead of building design) and the tools used are honed to address the effects of globalisation. The nations seem to dissolve.
A new 'order' is emerging based on agglomerations and dispersions. In this context of growing complexity it is necessary to find which methods or expedients could be adopted to best effect. It is necessary to construct accessible structures in order to comprehend and conceptualise the present and communicate it. The book can be seen as a 'manual' for the Regionmaker and describes the targets and the structure of the software.

Reading MVRDV, Nai Publishers, Rotterdam 2003
This book examines the context of MVRDV's research-based thinking and radical design strategies. It includes essays by Aaron Betsky, Bart Lootsma, Irénée Scalbert, Jean Attali, Stan Allen, Jos Bosman, Alain Guiheux, Philippe Morel, and Winy Maas. The contributors compare MVRDV with other generations and describe how new design concepts are born. The book was published on the occasion of the exhibition on the work of MVRDV held at the Netherlands Architecture Institute, the first in a series entitled 'NL Export'.

It later travelled to various institutes in Europe and the United States.
Five Minutes City, Episode Publishers, Rotterdam 2003
This study grew out of a forum and workshop held in Rotterdam in 2002 by Winy Maas, together with the Berlage Institute, the Institut Français d'Architecture, and the Fundació Mies van der Rohe on the theme of 'Architecture and [Im]mobility'.
The theme develops on the notion of *movement*: the world is in movement and those inhabiting it communicate and work faster and faster. People may change their country of residence any number of times during their lives for work or some other reason. All this requires a new technology of communication, a form of *access* aimed at improving the organisation of physical space, with immediate repercussions for architecture. The access requires social and political flexibility in planning, in real estate, and in architecture. What has to be created are structures, urban plans, and *modifiable* real estate. This objective could lead the world towards an incredible form of spatial acceleration.

KM3, Actar, Madrid 2005
It sprang from research developed with the Berlage Institute (1997–03) and critically examines the theme of *density*. Excessive development has profoundly transformed the traditional image of the country, leading to increased land

costs and stimulating the demand for increasingly greater investments. The studio proposes three-dimensional configurations (in the place of the traditional two-dimensional ones) that aim to recover new (unusual) possibilities for extra space; it is an '[…] attempt to create a utopian city that aims to anticipate the problems of world population increases and environmental protection' (Bart Lootsma, op. cit., p. 47). The study examines a set of projects and theoretical proposals formulated by MVRDV in the past ten years, analysing their spatial characteristics through 'three-dimensionality'. The book comprises a CD with software that aims to simulate infinite combinations on an architectonic and territorial scale.

Journals

El Croquis, no. 86/1997 and no. 111/2002
The two issues present forty projects, a good number of which have been built or are under construction. Both issues are accompanied by annotations, thoughts of the curators, and an interesting critical document represented by interviews with the three founders of MVRDV.

A+U Special Issue, Nov. 2002
An important monograph on MVRDV that seeks to give a complete overview of their work with fifty-nine projects completed over

eleven years. It also includes an outline of the group's future objectives.

Recognitions and prizes won by the studio

2005
Copenhagen City Buildings Prize for Frøsilos
Marcus Corporation Foundation Prize for overall work

2004
Amsterdam for Arts Prize 2003 for overall work

2003
Nominated for the Almere Architectuurprijs 2003 for the Top Tower in Almere
Finalist in the Mies van der Rohe for Contemporary Architecture Prize for Hageneiland

2002
NAi Prize 2002 Rotterdam (Netherlands Architecture Institute) for Hageneiland

2001
Dutch Pavilion Expo 2000 of Hannover selected for the European Union Prize for Contemporary Architecture – Mies van der Rohe Award
Nomination of the Dutch Pavilion Expo 2000 for the World Architecture Award as one of the five best Northern European projects

2000
Fritz Schumacher Prize for the overall work of MVRDV, Alfred Toepfer Foundation, Hannover, Germany
J.A. van Eckprijs awarded by BNA (Dutch Architects Association) first prize for WoZoCo's as a project built in the last five years

using strand board structures in a building, BNA, Amsterdam
Honourable Mention at the International Media Art Award for Mediacity/Datatown, Centre for Art and Mediatechnology, Karlsruhe, Germany

1999
Belmont Prize from the Forberg Schneider Foundation for the Dutch Pavilion Expo 2000
Finalist at the VI Mies van der Rohe Award for European Architecture for WoZoCo's

1998
Honourable Mention at the Nationale Staalprijs for Double House, Utrecht

1997
Concrete Award from Betonvereniging for Villa VPRO
Merkelbach Award from the Amsterdam Fund for Art for WoZoCo's
Dudok Award from the City of Hilversum for Villa VPRO
Finalist at the 1997 Mies van der Rohe Award for European Architecture for Three Porters' Lodges, Hoge Veluwe National Park

1996
Nomination for the Heuvelink Architecture Award Arnhem for Three Porters' Lodges

1993
Nomination for Art Incentive Award by the City of Amstelveen

1992
Nomination for the Frans Hals Award for exhibition design

List of Works

Photograph Credits

Hisao Suzuki
12, 16, 19, 22, 23, 24, 25, 27,
40, 43, 44, 45

Christian Richters
31, 32, 33, 34, 36, 37, 38, 39,
48, 49, 50

Studio MVRDV (H.W.)
46, 47

Michele Costanzo
53, 54, 56, 57

Robert Hart
66, 67, 69, 72, 75, 76, 77, 78,
79, 81, 83, 85, 87, 88-89, 95,
98-99, 100, 101, 113, 114-
115, 117, 119, 120, 121, 122,
123, 124-125, 126, 127, 138,
159, 160-161, 162, 163, 164,
165, 166, 167

*Farmax. Excursions
on Density*, 010 Publishers,
Rotterdam 1998, p. 41 58;
p. 541 61; p. 625 62;
p. 633 63

KM3, Actar, Madrid 2005,
p. 881 102; p. 841 108

Metacity/Datatown, 010
Publishers, Rotterdam,
1999, pp. 170-171 128

Costa Iberica, Actar,
Madrid 2000, p. 186 130;
p. 194 131

The other images are
by MVRDV's studio
and Michele Costanzo